GCSE English in a Week Language & Literature

For The Grade 9-1 Exams

www.How2Become.com

As part of this product you have also received FREE access to online tests that will help you to pass GCSE English assessments.

To gain access, simply go to:

www.MyEducationalTests.co.uk

Get more products for passing any test at:

www.How2Become.com

Orders: Please contact How2Become Ltd, Suite 3, 40 Churchill Square Business Centre, Kings Hill, Kent ME19 4YU.

You can order through Amazon.co.uk under ISBN: **9781912370290**, via the website www.How2Become.com or through Gardners.com.

ISBN: **9781912370290**

First published in 2018 by How2Become Ltd.

Copyright © 2018 How2Become.

All rights reserved. Apart from any permitted use under UK copyright law, no part of this publication may be reproduced or transmitted in any form or by any means, electronic or mechanical, including photocopying, recording, or any information, storage or retrieval system, without permission in writing from the publisher or under licence from the Copyright Licensing Agency Limited. Further details of such licenses (for reprographic reproduction) may be obtained from the Copyright Licensing Agency Ltd, Saffron House, 6-10 Kirby Street, London EC1N 8TS.

Typeset by Katie Noakes for How2Become Ltd.

Disclaimer

Every effort has been made to ensure that the information contained within this guide is accurate at the time of publication. How2Become Ltd is not responsible for anyone failing any part of any selection process as a result of the information contained within this guide. How2Become Ltd and their authors cannot accept any responsibility for any errors or omissions within this guide, however caused. No responsibility for loss or damage occasioned by any person acting, or refraining from action, as a result of the material in this publication can be accepted by How2Become Ltd.

The information within this guide does not represent the views of any third party service or organisation.

Contains public sector information licensed under the Open Government Licence v3.0.

CONTENTS

How to Use This Guide.. 9

GCSE English Literature Prep.. 13

GCSE English Literature Exam Structure.. 14

- *Breakdown of Assessments*.. 15
- *GCSE English Literature Grades 9-1*....................................... 19

GCSE English Language Prep... 21

GCSE English Language Exam Structure....................................... 22

- *Breakdown of Assessments*.. 24
- *GCSE English Language Grades 9-1*...................................... 26

A Chapter Full of Tips.. 29

English Preparation... 39

- *Grammar*.. 40
- *Punctuation*.. 43
- *Spelling*.. 46
- *How to Plan Your Answers*... 49
- *P.E.E.L*... 52
- *Superb Writing*... 53
- *Writing to Explain*... 58
- *Writing to Inform*.. 59
- *Writing to Describe*.. 60
- *Writing to Argue*... 61

- *Writing to Persuade* 62
- *Writing to Advise* 63
- *Day 1 Checklist* 64

Understanding Fiction 65

- *Types of Fiction* 66
- *Structure of Fiction Writing* 68
- *Setting, Atmosphere, Emotion* 69
- *Characters and Themes* 71
- *Imagery and Language* 72
- *Day 2 Checklist* 76

Understanding Non-Fiction 77

- *Structure of Non-Fiction Writing* 78
- *Essay Writing* 79
- *Story Writing* 83
- *Leaflets* 86
- *Letters* 87
- *Reviews* 88
- *Newspaper Articles* 89
- *Diaries* 91
- *Speeches* 92
- *Day 3 Checklist* 93

Works of Shakespeare 95

- *The Works of Shakespeare* 96

- *Theatre Performances*..105
- *Shakespearean Language*..107
- *Shakespeare's Use of Poetry in Drama*.. 112
- *Day 4 Checklist*... 113

Analysing Poetry..**115**
- *Analysing Poetry*... 116
- *Structure, Form, and Language*... 118
- *Poetic Techniques*... 123
- *Day 5 Checklist*..130

19th and 20th Century Prose..**131**
- *Day 6 Checklist*..134

Exam Practice..**135**
- *Suggested Comments*.. 151
- *Day 7 Checklist*..159

HOW TO USE THIS GUIDE

This guide comprises a full breakdown of the English exam for the GCSE English curriculum.

Not only have we provided you with a rundown of what to expect, how to prepare, and top tips for students and parents, but this book will help you to tailor your revision in just 7 days!

Take a look at the below structure to get an idea about how this guide will be formatted:

RECAP →
- GCSE English Literature Prep
- GCSE English Language Prep
- A Chapter Full of Tips

DAY 1 →
- Grammar, Punctuation, and Spelling
- Planning Your Answer
- Writing to Explain, Inform, and Describe
- Writing to Argue, Persuade, and Advise

DAY 2 →
- Understanding Fiction
- Setting, Atmosphere, and Emotion
- Characters and Themes
- Imagery and Language

DAY 3
- Understanding Non-Fiction
- Essays, Stories, and Letters
- Leaflets, Reviews, and Articles
- Diaries and Speeches

DAY 4
- Works of Shakespeare
- Theatre Performances
- Shakespearean Language
- Shakespeare's Use of Poetry

DAY 5
- Analysing Poetry
- Structure, Form, and Language
- Poetic Techniques

DAY 6
- 19th Century Prose
- 20th Century Prose

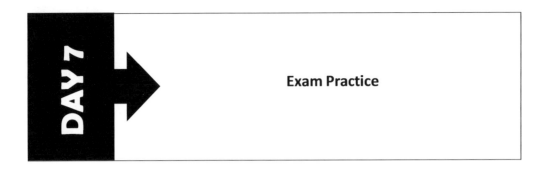

DAY 7 — Exam Practice

By following this 7-day plan, you will be able to work through your GCSE English exam structure in a clear, easy-to-follow format.

Whether you have left your revision to the last minute, or you simply want to brush up on all of your knowledge in the last week prior to the exam, this guide is the ideal resource for you. It will help you to fully comprehend the contents of your GCSE English exam, and hopefully pass with top marks!

GCSE ENGLISH LITERATURE PREP

GCSE ENGLISH LITERATURE EXAM STRUCTURE

Your GCSE Literature examination is comprised of **two** sections:

Paper 1: Shakespeare and the 19th Century novel

Marks out of 64

1 hour and 45 minutes

40% of GCSE

Paper 2: Modern texts and Poetry

Marks out of 96

2 hours and 15 minutes

60% of GCSE

Assessment Objectives

AO1 = To read, understand, and respond to literary texts. Students should be able to demonstrate a critical style in their writing, and develop an informed personal response. Students are also required to use contextual references, including quotations, in order to support their interpretation.

AO2 = To analyse the language, form, and structure used by an author and analyse the meaning and context. To ensure relevant terminology is used throughout their assessment.

AO3 = To show an understanding of the relationships between texts and the contexts in which a piece of text is written.

AO4 = To use an array of vocabulary and sentence structures in order to provide clarity, purpose and effect, with accurate spelling and punctuation.

Weighting of Assessment Objectives

Below we have outlined the weighting of assessment objectives for your GCSE English Literature exam.

AOs	Paper 1 (approx)	Paper 2 (approx)	Overall weighting (approx)
AO1	15	22.5	37.5
AO2	15	27.5	42.5
AO3	7.5	7.5	15
AO4	2.5	2.5	5
Overall weighting of components	40%	60%	100%

BREAKDOWN OF ASSESSMENTS

Before you begin preparing for each section of your GCSE English Literature exam, we think it is important that you understand what to expect in terms of subject content, and how to make the most out of your revision time.

Shakespeare

During the Shakespeare section of your English Literature exam, you will be required to answer **ONE** question.

Students will study one play within the classroom, and therefore, the choice of question you should answer should be the one you have been focusing on during your English lessons.

In the exam, there will be a choice of six possible Shakespeare plays. The following texts are examples taken from the 2017 examination:

- *Macbeth;*
- *Romeo and Juliet;*
- *The Tempest;*
- *The Merchant of Venice;*
- *Much Ado About Nothing;*
- *Julius Caesar.*

PLEASE NOTE: The choice of Shakespearean texts is subject to change annually. Be sure to check with your teacher with regards to the Shakespeare text that you will be studying!

The 19th Century Novel

During the 19th Century novel section of your English Literature exam, you will be required to answer **ONE** question.

Students will study one novel within the classroom, so the choice of question you should answer should be the one you have been focusing on during your English lessons.

In the exam, there will be a choice of seven novels. The following texts are examples taken from the 2017 examination:

- *The Strange Case of Dr Jekyll and Mr Hyde;*
- *A Christmas Carol;*
- *Great Expectations;*
- *Jane Eyre;*
- *Frankenstein;*
- *Pride and Prejudice;*
- *The Sign of Four.*

PLEASE NOTE: The choice of 19th Century texts are subject to change annually. Be sure to check with your teacher with regards to the novel that you will be studying!

Modern Texts

During the modern text section of your English Literature exam, you will be required to answer **ONE** question.

Students will study one text within the classroom, so the choice of question you should answer should be the one you have been focusing on during your English lessons.

In the exam, there will be a choice of twelve texts, including post-1914 prose and drama. The following texts are examples taken from the 2017 examination:

PROSE

Author	Title
William Golding	*Lord of the Flies*
AQA Anthology	*Telling Tales*
George Orwell	*Animal Farm*
Kazuo Ishiguro	*Never Let Me Go*
Meera Syal	*Anita and Me*
Stephen Kelman	*Pigeon English*

DRAMA

Author	Title
JB Priestley	*An Inspector Calls*
Willy Russell	*Blood Brothers*
Alan Bennett	*The History Boys*
Dennis Kelly	*DNA*
Simon Stephens	*The Curious Incident of the Dog in the Night-Time*
Shelagh Delaney	*A Taste of Honey*

PLEASE NOTE: The choice of modern texts is subject to change annually. Be sure to check with your teacher with regards to the novel/play that you will be studying!

Poetry

During the poetry section of your English Literature exam, you will be required to answer **ONE CLUSTER OF POEMS** in the exam.

The poems assessed in the exam will be taken from the AQA poetry anthology, *Poems Past and Present*.

In the exam, there will be a choice of two clusters, each containing 15 poems. The poems in each cluster are thematically linked.

The themes provided for the 2017 examinations were the following:

- Love and Relationships;
- Power and Conflict.

For this section of the exam, students need to study all 15 poems in their chosen cluster and be prepared to write about any of them in the exam.

PLEASE NOTE: The choice of poetry texts and themes are subject to change annually. Be sure to check with your teacher with regards to the poems/themes that you will be studying!

Unseen Poetry

The unseen poetry section of your English Literature exam is self-explanatory. This section will provide poems which you will not have studied during your English lessons.

The best way to revise for the unseen poetry section is to experience a wide range of poetry and develop the following analytical skills:

CONTENT	THEMES
LANGUAGE	**STRUCTURE**

GCSE ENGLISH LITERATURE GRADES 9-1

As of 2017, the GCSE grading system for the English subject uses a 9-1 scoring criteria.

Based on this new scoring system, students should be aiming for a Grade 9 – the highest possible grade, currently set at a higher level than what an A* used to be.

By 2019, all GCSE subjects will use this new and improved grading system with the hope to provide more differentiation between students' scores.

Below we have provided a diagram outlining the new 9-1 grading system, just to give you some insight into how this compares to the old A*-U grading system.

Average %	85+	69-84	46-68		32-45	15-31	Under 15
New grading system	9	8	7	6	5	4	3
Old grading system	A*		A	B	C	D	E

PLEASE NOTE: the above scoring system does not necessarily reflect the actual grading system of all exam boards and should be used as a guideline only. It is recommended to check with your exam board for their exact scoring system.

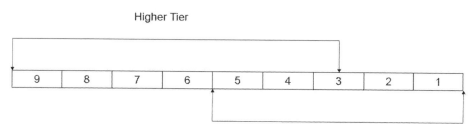

Higher Tier

Foundation Tier

GCSE ENGLISH LANGUAGE PREP

GCSE ENGLISH LANGUAGE EXAM STRUCTURE

Your GCSE Language examination is comprised of **two** sections:

Paper 1: Explorations in Creative Reading and Writing

Marks out of 80

1 hour and 45 minutes

50% of GCSE

Paper 2: Writers' Viewpoints and Perspectives

Marks out of 80

1 hour and 45 minutes

50% of GCSE

Assessment Objectives

AO1 = To identify and interpret information and ideas, and select evidence from different texts.

AO2 = To explain, comment on, and analyse how writers use language and structure in order to affect and influence.

AO3 = To compare writers' ideas and perspectives and demonstrate how they are conveyed through different texts.

AO4 = To evaluate texts critically and support your answers using examples and evidence from different texts.

AO5 = To communicate effectively and imaginatively, using tone and style. Organise writing in a clear, structured manner to create coherence throughout your answers.

AO6 = To use a range of vocabulary and terminology in order to enhance your writing and show your knowledge. This includes grammar, punctuation, and spelling.

AO7 = Demonstrate presentation skills in a formal written setting.

AO8 = To listen and respond to spoken language.

AO9 = Use spoken standard English effectively.

Weighting of Assessment Objectives

Below we have outlined the weighting of assessment objectives for your GCSE English Language exam.

AOs	Paper 1 (approx)	Paper 2 (approx)	Overall weighting (approx)
AO1	2.5%	7.5%	10%
AO2	10%	7.5%	17.5%
AO3	N/A	10%	10%
AO4	12.5%	N/A	12.5%
AO5	15%	15%	30%
AO6	10%	10%	20%
Overall weighting of components	50%	50%	100%

BREAKDOWN OF ASSESSMENTS

Before you begin preparing for each section of your GCSE English Language exam, we think it is important that you understand what to expect in terms of subject content, and how to make the most out of your revision time.

Paper 1

During Paper 1 of your English Language exam, you will be required to answer **ALL FIVE** questions.

In the exam, you will be provided with an extract from a work of literary fiction. This will either be from the 20th or 21st century.

Below we have included a breakdown of the questions you will face in Paper 1:

Question	Details
Question 1	This question is worth 4 marks and you should spend about 5 minutes on this.
Question 2	This question is worth 8 marks and you should spend about 10 minutes on this.
Question 3	This question is worth 8 marks and you should spend about 10 minutes on this.
Question 4	This question is worth 20 marks and you should spend about 20 minutes on this.
Question 5	This question is worth 40 marks and you should spend about 45 minutes on this.

PLEASE NOTE: The choice of literary fiction is subject to change annually.

Paper 2

During Paper 2 of your English Language exam, you will be required to answer **ALL FIVE** questions.

In the exam, you will be provided with two non-fiction extracts – one from the 19th century and one from either the 20th or 21st century.

Below we have included a breakdown of the questions you will face in Paper 2:

Question	Details
Question 1	This question is worth 4 marks and you should spend about 5 minutes on this.
Question 2	This question is worth 8 marks and you should spend about 8 minutes on this.
Question 3	This question is worth 12 marks and you should spend about 12 minutes on this.
Question 4	This question is worth 16 marks and you should spend about 20 minutes on this.
Question 5	This question is worth 40 marks and you should spend about 45 minutes on this.

PLEASE NOTE: The choice of literary fiction is subject to change annually.

GCSE ENGLISH LANGUAGE GRADES 9-1

As of 2017, the GCSE grading system for the English exam uses a 9-1 scoring criteria.

Based on this new scoring system, students should be aiming for a Grade 9 – the highest possible grade, currently set at a higher level than what an A* used to be.

By 2019, all GCSE subjects will use this new and improved grading system with the hope to provide more differentiation between students' scores.

Below we have provided a diagram outlining the new 9-1 grading system, just to give you some insight into how this compares to the old A*-U grading system.

Average %	85+	69-84	46-68	32-45	15-31	Under 15
New grading system	9	8	7	6	5	4	3
Old grading system	A*	A	B	C	D	E

PLEASE NOTE: the above scoring system does not necessarily reflect the actual grading system of all exam boards and should be used as a guideline only. It is recommended to check with your exam board for their exact scoring system.

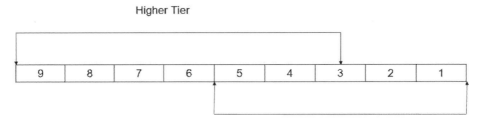

In order to increase your chances of securing top marks in your English GCSE, we suggest you take a look at our other guides to help you on your way to acing your GCSE!

A CHAPTER FULL OF TIPS

Not only do we think its important to learn about the structure and content of your exam, but we also think it practical that you revise some top tips and soak up some of the best exam advice prior to commencing your revision.

Tip 1 – Find out as much as you can!

Before your exam, you should find out as much information as you can about what you'll face on the day.

Below are some of the most essential things that you SHOULD know before undergoing your revision:

- The examination board;
- The subject content;
- The books to be focusing on;
- Understanding how much each section is worth (in percentage).

Tip 2 – Create a timetable

It is important that every minute leading up to your exam should be spent wisely and effectively.

The best way to do this is to create a timetable for yourself and try to adhere to it as much as possible.

On the following page, we have created a sample timetable that you can fill out according to your Literature exam. Be sure to factor in time for each section of the paper – Shakespeare, 19th-century prose, modern texts, and poetry.

	Mon	Tues	Wed	Thurs	Fri	Sat	Sun
9am – 10am							
10am – 11am							
11am – 12pm							
12pm – 1pm							
1pm – 2pm							

	Mon	Tues	Wed	Thurs	Fri	Sat	Sun
2pm – 3pm							
3pm – 4pm							
4pm – 5pm							
5pm – 6pm							
6pm – 7pm							

A Chapter Full of Tips

Tip 3 – Practise grammar, punctuation, and spelling

Sadly, revising for English can be a bit of a pain. Outside of practising your spelling, grammar, and handwriting, the best way to get better at English essays is to write them. Preferably, you should try to write these under exam conditions, using the same timings as those in the real exam.

Tip 4 – Learn the material

The first step to success at English GCSE is to know what you're talking about. Make sure you read the books, plays, or poems that you need to answer questions on in the exam. If it helps, find film adaptations which are faithful to the original material – this can help you visualise the events of the novel or play more easily.

On top of this, there are plenty of websites and books which offer interpretations and critiques of the texts that you're studying. You can use these as a guide to the text, or as arguments in your essays.

For plays and novels, you should try to remember the key events which take place, as well as the main characters and their personalities. Creating a small fact file with profiles for each character can be a fun way of summarising them and their role in the text. If it helps, you can even use descriptions of the characters' looks to sketch them, giving you a broader picture of what they would be like.

For the story, try to reduce the book into the key events. Preferably, try to find the three key events of the text – the ones which define its three acts. Then, reduce these three chunks into three smaller events, meaning that you have nine events which drive the plot of the novel or play. You can then sort these events into a flowchart so that you can easily remember the order of events.

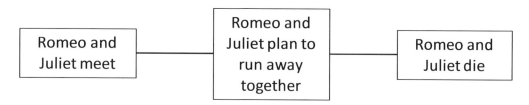

From here, the nine key events could be:

1. Romeo and Juliet attend the ball.
2. Romeo and Juliet meet.
3. The balcony scene occurs.

4. Romeo meets with Friar Lawrence to make wedding arrangements.
5. Lord Capulet arranges for Juliet to marry Paris.
6. Romeo kills Tybalt and is banished.

7. Juliet takes the drug to feign her death.
8. Romeo drinks the poison upon finding Juliet 'dead' in her tomb.
9. Juliet awakens to find Romeo's body, then takes her own life.

Finally, you will need to remember the core themes for the novel, play, or poem. Generally, the texts you study will have one or two primary themes (in the case of *Romeo and Juliet*, these might be 'love' and 'fate'). In addition to this, there may be a few minor themes. Additional reading of secondary sources, such as literary criticism, will reveal some of these ideas. Experiment with different revision techniques which suit you in order to remember the key themes of the text, as well as key events, characters, or lines of the text which relate to them.

Sadly, English at GCSE often requires you to remember key quotes. This can be annoying, but the best way to learn them is to read them, write them or listen to them being spoken over and over until they stick in your head.

Tip 5 – Answer practice questions

Once you're confident that you know all of the different characters, story events, and themes of your text, it's time to get to work on practice questions. As usual, get hold of some past papers and answer all of the questions that are relevant to your course.

If you get tired of writing whole essays, then at least you can attempt writing essay plans for them. This will still test your knowledge and ability to structure an answer, even if it doesn't completely match the experience of writing a full essay.

The most difficult part of using practice questions to revise for English is that you will need to find someone to read and mark your essay, so that you know where you're doing well, and where you need to improve. Ask your teacher if it's possible for them to take a look at your essays or essay plans, and they might be able to give you some pointers, giving you a rough idea of what to work on next.

Tip 6 – Read the mark scheme

Unlike the mark schemes for Maths and Science, which contain right or wrong answers, the marking criteria for English exams is a bit more abstract. In an English exam, you aren't necessarily being marked on what your argument is, but rather how well you argue it, and how clear your message is. This is reflected in the mark scheme, where clarity in writing and how robust your argument is are valued most. Take a look at the mark schemes for the exams that you're sitting to see exactly what is being asked of you.

Tip 7 – Practise your handwriting

Handwriting is vital because the examiner needs to be able to read what you have written in order to mark it accurately. If the examiner can't read your work, they won't mark it. Therefore, you should spend some time practising handwriting if you think yours isn't up to standard. You'll probably be writing very quickly in the exam, which means that your handwriting will probably be less legible than usual. Doing practice essays is a good way to find ways of making your handwriting neater, especially if you do the mock exams under timed conditions. If it helps, cut out joined-up handwriting in favour of print handwriting, so that the examiner is more likely to be able to understand what words you've written.

Tip 8 – Always have a plan

When it comes to success at English GCSE, the most valuable thing is to plan your essay before you begin. Once you open your exam paper, you might find a question that's perfect. You might be tempted to go head-first into your answer because you want to secure the marks, but it pays to exercise restraint and take the question more slowly. The length of the exam is designed to allow students to write a quick plan before starting each question, so you won't be losing time to spend on your essay if you take a moment to write a plan. In fact, planning will make your time much more valuable, since you'll have a good idea of what direction your answer is going in.

Planning your answer is beneficial for two reasons. Firstly, it'll force you to look at the question more closely. This means that you'll answer the actual question in the paper, rather than misinterpret it or create a question in your head that you would like to answer. Many students fail to answer the question directly, and planning will help you clarify what's being asked of you in the exam.

A plan will also help you stick to the point of the essay. As you write an answer, you can slowly drift away from the main point and get side-tracked by minor details which aren't entirely relevant to the question. Staying relevant is vital when doing your English exams. You don't have enough time to talk about everything surrounding a book, play, poem or other topic, so you need to focus on exactly what the question is asking. When you write your plan, you can list details which are strictly relevant, and cut out anything you don't need.

Tip 9 – Make a point, provide evidence, then explain it

This is one of the best ways to structure your answers in an English exam, or any other test which is essay-based, and requires you to form an argument. However, this method won't work for the creative writing exercises.

1. **MAKE YOUR POINT** – Here, you need to make a claim which relates to the question. For example, "One of the main themes in *Romeo and Juliet* is fate."

2. **PROVIDE EVIDENCE** – Depending on what exam you are sitting, the type of evidence you provide might change. For an English exam, you're likely to take a quote from the text, for example, "A pair of star-cross'd lovers take their life."

3. **EXPLAIN IT** – Finally, you need to link your evidence to the

point that you've made. In this case, you might say "the phrase 'star-cross'd' implies that Romeo and Juliet were destined to meet each other for a brief moment in time, only to be pulled away from each other in death."

This method is excellent for structuring an argument, and can work throughout an essay. Remember to always link your argument to the question by saying something along the lines of "this relates to the question because…". This shows the examiner that you understand how what you are writing relates to the overall topic. For extra marks, you can show how your points link to one another as well, showing that you have a more complete picture of what you are writing about.

Tip 10 – Learn the best revision techniques for you

There are three major ways that people revise and absorb information. These are:

- **VISUAL** – This involves using visual aids such as note-taking and creative mapping of information, to commit things to memory.
- **AURAL** – The use of videos, music or other recordings to allow information to sink in.
- **KINAESTHETIC** – Using activities which involve interaction, to remember key details (such as flashcards and revision games).

Different paths will work better for different people, but also bear in mind that certain subjects will also suit these methods differently.

Essentially, you will need to experiment with different styles in order to find which ones best suit you, but you will also need to discover what works for each of your subjects.

Tip 11 – Ease into it

Before you start, revision can feel like a huge mountain, impossible to climb to the top of. It can be incredibly daunting. You might be overwhelmed by the feeling that you are completely unprepared and don't know enough. That said, you need to make a start sometime. Some revision is better than no revision at all, so if you're struggling to get started with your studies, ease your way into it. Start by revising for a much shorter period of time, and maybe focus on the things that you already know well or most enjoy. Once you're comfortable and confident, move onto something that you're less sure of.

Tip 12 – Treat yourself

Make sure you keep yourself motivated with some treats. You don't need to go overboard, but the "carrot and stick" method of revision can keep you working for longer periods of time, allowing you to get through more work. Things like "I'll get some ice cream, but only after I've done the next 3 pages" are a great way of keeping you going and keeping your spirits up.

Tip 13 – Think ahead

Finally, always think ahead past exams. Life continues after your GCSEs, and you'll be treated to an extra-long summer once you've finished. You might feel that you're not in a great place while revising, that your social life is suffering or your free time is being eaten up by studies, but it will all be worth it when you get great results. This positive outlook – thinking towards the future – is one of the best ways to get you started with revision, and keep you going with it too.

ENGLISH PREPARATION
Day 1

GRAMMAR

When it comes to grammar, you need to try and avoid silly grammatical mistakes.

In order to do this, you need to brush up on your grammar skills. Below we have provided you with lots of grammar techniques that you SHOULD already know. However, you can use this chapter to brush up on your knowledge.

For each grammar technique, we have provided you space so that you can write down the correct definition along with an example. We have done the first one for you.

GRAMMAR	DEFINITION	EXAMPLE
Articles	*An article is used usually before a noun.*	*'A', 'an' and 'the' are all examples of an article.*
Prepositions		
Conjunctions		

DAY 1 ➡ **English Preparation**

GRAMMAR	DEFINITION	EXAMPLE
Adjectives		
Verbs		
Adverbs		
Nouns		
Pronouns		

DAY 1 → **English Preparation**

GRAMMAR	DEFINITION	EXAMPLE
Simple sentences		
Compound sentences		
Complex sentences		

In your GCSE Exam, or for any exam for that matter, you will be marked on your grammar, punctuation, and spelling.

We recommend that you pay attention to your grammar, particularly when it comes to your Language paper. You will lose easy marks if you show little to no understanding of English grammar.

Now that we've had a look at some of the key terminologies in relation to grammar, let's move on to punctuation.

DAY 1 → English Preparation

PUNCTUATION

Punctuation is just as important as grammar.

From capital letters and full stops to apostrophes and question marks, there are a range of literary punctuation techniques that you need to be aware of.

For each punctuation device, we have provided you space so that you can write down the correct definition along with an example. We have done the first one for you.

PUNCTUATION	DEFINITION	EXAMPLE
Capital letters	A capital letter is used to begin sentences. They are also used for proper nouns.	Proper nouns include names of places such as Buckingham Palace.
Full stops		
Ellipses		

DAY 1 ➡ **English Preparation**

44 GCSE English in a Week

PUNCTUATION	DEFINITION	EXAMPLE
Commas ,		
Inverted commas " "		
Exclamation marks !		
Question marks ?		
Apostrophes '		

DAY 1 → English Preparation

PUNCTUATION	DEFINITION	EXAMPLE
Colons :		
Semi-colons ;		
Brackets ( )		
Dashes —		
Hyphens -		

DAY 1 → **English Preparation**

SPELLING

Spelling is crucial in your writing for both the English Literature and English Language exams.

Spelling is relatively straightforward but is just as important as the grammar and punctuation elements of your exam. Ensure that your spelling is at its very best to ensure that you don't lose marks when it comes to grammar, punctuation, and spelling.

Below we have included some key terms in relation to spelling. We have provided space for you to write the definition and your own examples to help you remember the key terms.

SPELLING	DEFINITION	EXAMPLE
Homophones		
Homonyms		
Tenses		

DAY 1 ➡ **English Preparation**

English Preparation

SPELLING	DEFINITION	EXAMPLE
The 'I' before 'E' except after 'C' rule		
Silent letters		
Unstressed letters		
Singular vs. plural spellings		
Prefixes vs. suffixes		

DAY 1 ➤ **English Preparation**

COMMONLY MISSPELT WORDS

Below we have included a list of some of the most commonly misspelt words. Be sure that you learn these off by heart.

Accommodate	Achieve	Acquire	Argument
Calendar	Convenience	Definite	Desperate
Disappoint	Environment	Exaggerate	Foreign
Government	Happiness	Humorous	Laboratory
Necessary	Occasion	Occurred	Parallel
Perceive	Privilege	Professional	Recommend
Rhythm	Separate	Succeed	Twelfth

If there are particular words you struggle with, we suggest that you create your own list in the space provided.

DAY 1 → English Preparation

HOW TO PLAN YOUR ANSWERS

Now that you've grasped the nature of the exam and what to expect from the questions, it's time to learn how to plan your answers.

Thoroughly read the question

Before you do anything, it is important that you read through the questions **CAREFULLY.**

1. Allow yourself 10 to 15 minutes to read through the questions and the texts before you begin answering the questions.

2. Before you read each text, make sure that you have a good understanding about what the question is asking of you. Keep this in mind when you read through the text.

3. A great way to plan your answer is to highlight any keywords or phrases as you go. Not only will this save time in the long run, but it will allow you to pinpoint key topics that you might want to talk about in your answer.

Don't dive straight in

The most important thing to remember when it comes to writing, is to take your time and plan what you are going to say.

Examiners will know if you have structured your response beforehand.

Make notes

Before you start writing, take some time to jot down some key bullet points and ideas.

1. You don't need to spend too long on this – just get some ideas and points down that you think may help you when answering the

question.

2. Making notes and planning your answers are necessary for the longer exam questions that are worth more marks. If the question is more about fact-finding, a simple highlighting process will work just as well for planning your answer.

Mind-mapping

Although this comes under note-taking, we think that mind-mapping deserves a mention on its own. Mind-mapping is a fantastic way of planning your answer. It allows you to organise your ideas and link them by themes, motives, language, structure, etc.

Visually representing your notes allows you to have a clear focus on how to structure your response. Generally, a central concept appears in the centre of a page, and then other details spread away from it. This is excellent for quickly jotting down all of the information you can remember, and then organising it into sections.

Take a look at the following example:

- The foundation of Othello and Desdemona's relationship is passion, not love.
- Othello believes that love in marriage takes time to develop.
- Desdemona's platonic love to Cassio is misinterpreted by Othello as sexual love.

- Desdemona's father sees Othello marrying Desdemona as theft of some kind of property.
- The mixed-race marriage between Othello and Desdemona would've been unusual and likely the target of prejudice and scrutiny.
- The two married women in the play (Desdemona and Emilia) are wrongfully accused of adultery.

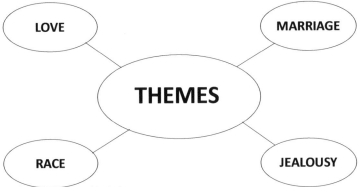

- Othello is a black man in a high position in the Venetian military, which would have been unusual for the time.
- Iago uses suspicions about Othello and Desdemona's mixed-race marriage to his advantage.
- Othello has internalised some of this racial prejudice, believing himself to be unworthy of Desdemona's love.

- Iago warns Othello of jealousy being a "green-eyed monster".
- Iago himself has experienced jealousy via his relationship with Emilia.
- Othello's jealousy clouds his judgement, despite him once being a calm and collected individual.

DAY 1 ➡ English Preparation

As you can see, the mind-map allows you to draw comparisons and make links between different ideas. By organising your notes like this, you will be in a far stronger position to tackle your essay questions in the literature exam.

PROS	CONS
Can be made by hand or computer	Not effective for some subjects/topics
Can be a great way of improving handwriting	Has the potential to be less efficient and more time-consuming than other methods such as note-taking
Forces you to write incredibly concise notes, which is great for remembering	Not necessarily an excellent method if you aren't particulary creative
Excellent for subjects with lots of connected concepts	
Allows you to be creative which can alleviate some stress	
Excellent for memory since you can visually recall the entire mind map in your head	

Once you've planned your answers, it's now time to think about how you're actually going to write them. To get the highest marks, we suggest that you use the writing technique, **P.E.E.L**, to structure your response.

Keep your notes simple

- Try not to ramble on.
- Keep your notes on point, focused, and short.
- The snappier your notes are, the easier they are to remember.
- Think of keywords and phrases.

DAY 1 ➡ **English Preparation**

Know what you want to say

- Before you begin writing, you will need to know **ROUGHLY** what it is you want to say.
- What main points do you want to cover?
- What is the purpose of the text?
- Who is going to be reading the text?
- Consider what you want to achieve from your written text.

P.E.E.L

In order to secure top marks, you need to structure your responses like so:

Point = What is the point you are trying to make?

Example = Give an example from the text to support your point.

Explanation = Explain how your example supports your point.

Link = Link your point to further evidence, or explain the significance between the point and context in which it's written.

There are different versions of the P.E.E.L. technique.

P.E.E.D	P.E.E.R	P.E.E.C.E
Point. Example. Evidence. Develop.	Point. Example. Explain. Relate.	Point. Example. Explain. Compare. Explore.

We advise that you use the one that you've been taught.

DAY 1 ➡ English Preparation

SUPERB WRITING

Not only do you have to master the art of exams and have the correct knowledge, but you also need to be able to demonstrate that knowledge through superb writing.

Even if you have grasped all the right concepts and your overall response to the question is good, this also needs to be reflected in how well you write.

IT'S NOT JUST WHAT YOU WRITE, BUT HOW WELL YOU WRITE!

Below we have provided some of the basic, but most important things you should remember with regards to your writing.

Structure

Essays are a great way to structure your writing. Essays are a form of writing which allow you to answer a question.

WHAT ALL GOOD ESSAYS NEED

All good essays need a clear and focused structure. You can achieve this by creating an introduction, a middle, and an end.

INTRODUCTION

- Outline what direction your response is going to take;
- You could include a hypothesis;
- Use keywords from the question;
- 2-3 sentences is sufficient for an introduction;
- The reader should be able to read your introduction and conclusion, and know what your essay is about.

MAIN BODY

- Answer the question by making 3-4 points;
- Support these points with examples, quotes, and analysis;
- Make sure you keep referring to the question;
- 3-4 paragraphs is sufficient for an essay;
- Analyse and explain key points, their relevance, and your opinions.

CONCLUSION

- Summarise the key points you've made and how they are important/relevant;
- DO NOT introduce any new points at this point;
- Make sure you write a sentence referring to the question;
- The reader should be able to read your introduction and conclusion, and know what your essay is about.

Essay features

As well as structure, essays also need to flow, use effective language, use the correct tone, and of course, answer the question.

Essay Features	Explanation
Language	Consider what language is best. For essays, formal and technical language is great. Only use vocabulary that you know the meaning of.
Tone and Style	You need to set the tone. Is it a serious or light-hearted essay? Your language should reflect this.
Paragraphing	Use a paragraph for each new point. Your introduction and conclusion will form paragraphs, and you should have 3 or 4 paragraphs to complete the bulk of your essay.

Literary techniques	Avoid repetition. Rhetorical questions are great to interact with your reader. Consider what techniques you can use to enhance your writing (metaphors, personifcation, etc.)

Choice of words and phrases

When it comes to writing your response, it's handy to have an array of words and phrases that you can use.

Below we have incorporated a list of words and phrases that you should try to remember for **ALL** of your essays:

- In other words...
- In order to...
- To put it another way...
- This highlights...
- This signifies...
- This reflects...
- Furthermore...
- Moreover...
- Similarly...
- Another key thing to remember...
- Not only...but also...
- Coupled with...
- Not to mention...
- Firstly, secondly, thirdly...
- Having said that...
- Then again...

- That said...
- Alternatively...
- Conversely...
- In the same way...
- In addition...
- In comparison...
- For instance...
- With this in mind...
- Provided that...
- In light of...
- In view of...
- Nevertheless...
- Significantly...
- Notably...
- Above all...
- In conclusion...
- All things considered...

DAY 1 ➡ **English Preparation**

Grammar, Punctuation, Spelling, and Handwriting

Not only will you be awarded for correct answers, but marks are also up for grabs with regards to grammar, punctuation, spelling, and handwriting.

GRAMMAR

1. Be careful using *its* and *it's*.
2. Be careful when using *their*, *there* and *they're*.
3. Don't change between tenses.
4. Avoid double negatives (E.g. there *wasn't no* evidence).
5. Brush up on the definitions of: adjectives, nouns, verbs, prepositions, etc.
6. Start a new paragraph for every new point.

PUNCTUATION

1. Make sure to use capital letters and full stops.
2. Brush up on the definitions of: commas, colons, semi-colons, exclamation marks, ellipses, etc.
3. Use apostrophes correctly.
4. Include quotation marks where applicable.

SPELLING

1. Always write words out in full as opposed to abbreviations (etc. or e.g.)
2. Any evidence taken from the text should be spelt and punctuated exactly how it appears.
3. Make sure that any literary technique name you use, is spelt correctly (onomatopoeia).
4. If you are unsure about how to spell a word, consider using a different word.

DAY 1 ➡ English Preparation

HANDWRITING

Legible handwriting is crucial in assessments, especially in an English assessment. Poor handwriting might hinder your chances of securing marks if the examiner is unable to read your writing.

Most exam papers are scanned electronically and examiners read the papers on-screen. That means your handwriting needs to be as clear as possible to ensure readability.

1. Be sure to use the correct colour pen. Most exams now request that you write your answers in a black pen.
2. Try to write as neatly as possible to make it easier to read.
3. If you make a mistake, neatly cross it out and write it again.
4. Practise prior to your exams. Handwriting can be easily improved the more you practice it.

WRITING TO EXPLAIN

EXPLAIN  EXPLANATION

When you are writing to explain, you will provide information that is factual.

FOR EXAMPLE:

Explain the importance of exercise.

- For this question, you need to provide facts about why exercise is important.
- You will do this by providing reasons, examples and analysis to justify your response.

Useful techniques in explanative writing:

- Generally written in third person;
- Written in past or present tense;
- Use connectives to compare;
- Clear, factual language;
- Use examples and evidence to support your writing.

WRITING TO INFORM

| INFORM | = | INFORMATION |

When you are writing to inform, you would provide the basic facts. The main difference between informing and explaining, is that explanations require more detail.

FOR EXAMPLE:

Inform the students about school uniform policies.

- Basic, straightforward language to convey the key information about school uniform policies.
- Give information about what the school uniform policies are, and why they're important.

Useful techniques in informative writing:

- Clear, factual, and informal;
- Information should be impersonal;
- Provide facts through examples and statistics;
- Consider what, where, when, how, and why;
- Language should reflect the mood and genre of the text.

WRITING TO DESCRIBE

Generally, writing to describe will draw upon emotions and feelings.

FOR EXAMPLE:

Describe a setting by the lake.

- Describe the lake using adjectives and emotive language.
- Consider how the lake makes you feel. Draw upon your senses – sight, sound, smell, taste, touch.

Useful techniques in descriptive writing:

- Strong use of adjectives;
- Use of similes, metaphors, personification, pathetic fallacy, hyperbole etc.;
- Senses – sight, sound, touch, taste, smell;
- Emotive language – create an emotional response;
- Allow your readers to visualise characters and settings.

WRITING TO ARGUE

When it comes to writing, sometimes you will be required to write in a particular format.

WRITING TO ARGUE

Writing to argue is a piece of writing where you argue a particular point.

Arguments in writing are very different from verbal arguments. In verbal arguments, you can be passionate and say what you want. Whereas, in writing, you still need to remain structured and formal.

GAPS	EXPLANATION
G – genre	What kind of writing document are you writing? (Letters, article, speech, story). Whatever form of writing you use, you will need to adhere to the conventions.
A – audience	Who is your targeted audience? Consider age group and what kind of language and style you need to use in order to appeal to your reader.
P – purpose	For argument texts, you need to change the minds of your readers. The keyword to remember is **influence**.
S – style	Informal vs. formal. Again, this will depend on your audience.

Things to consider:

- Consider both views of the argument;
- You need to write a rational well-balanced argument using descriptions and explanations;
- Emphasise your points by making them sound really good;
- Facts and statistics are great to use in writing;
- Dismiss opposing views.

WRITING TO PERSUADE

Writing to persuade uses similar techniques as writing to argue. Both of these styles of writing require you to influence your reader.

Generally, when writing to persuade, you don't have to offer alternative viewpoints; you simply have to present your own ideas.

> ### FOR EXAMPLE:
>
> **How would you persuade someone to buy a new pair of running trainers?**
>
> - You would need to work out who your audience is;
> - You would need to use emotive language to appeal to the reader;
> - You would need to use evidence and support your reasoning (i.e. comfort, price, durable, high quality etc.);
> - You would need to be positive in your way of writing;
> - You would need to be personal;
> - Language is your ammunition to sell the product;
> - Exaggerate your points but DO NOT lie;
> - Compare it to your competitors and say how yours is better.

PLAY ON YOUR READER'S EMOTIONS

A great piece of persuasive writing will use expressive language to emphasise key points and persuade the reader/audience to buy, or consider something.

You need to exert yourself and make your writing sound impressive! Repeat things, use questions and statistics, be personal and use feelings to get your viewpoints across!

DAY 1 ➡ English Preparation

WRITING TO ADVISE

If you are asked to write a text to advise on something, this basically means that you need to offer your opinion and ideas.

This is a much gentler way of writing as opposed to written arguments or persuasive texts.

FOR EXAMPLE:

A school is trying to raise money for a charity close to their hearts. You are asked to advise the children on ideas about fundraising, and what needs to be done.

- Offer your personal opinions. You don't have to give definitive reasons, but friendly suggestions and advice.
- Instead of using words like "should" or "will", you should use words like "could" or "might". This demonstrates that you are simply offering help.
- Focus on an idea you could use (i.e. car washes, bake sales etc.) and show how you could run the event smoothly.
- You can consider more than one option. Advising someone means offering ideas and opinions.

Your writing should be gentle, soft, and friendly. You are NOT making commands; instead you are offering suggestions.

Day 1 Checklist

You have now completed your Day 1 revision.

How confident are you feeling?

Below we have included a checklist that you can tick off to make sure that you have learnt everything regarding this chapter.

I feel fully prepared with regards to my English preperation. ☐

I have studied a range of grammar techniques that I feel confident in tackling. ☐

I have studied a range of punctuation techniques that I feel confident in tackling. ☐

I have studied a range of spelling techniques that I feel confident in tackling. ☐

I have read and understood the information on how to plan my answers effectively. ☐

I have learned how to improve my writing to ensure higher marks in my GCSE English exam. ☐

DAY 1 ➡ **Checklist**

UNDERSTANDING FICTION
Day 2

TYPES OF FICTION

There are three types of fiction texts that may appear in your GCSE Language exam:

- *Prose;*
- *Poetry;*
- *Plays.*

What is fiction?

Fiction is the creation of stories and ideas. They are created by the IMAGINATION.

These stories did NOT happen in real life.

Types of fiction

There are many different types, or genres, of fiction:

FANTASY	ROMANCE	HORROR	SCIENCE-FICTION
MYSTERY	REALISTIC	HISTORICAL	FOLKTALES
ADVENTURE	SPORTS	HUMOUR	CLASSICS

The narrative

When reading a story it is important, as the reader, to be drawn into the mind-set of the author. For the moments you sit there reading, you want to be able to escape from real life and enter a world full of fantasy and make-believe.

DAY 2 ➡ Understanding Fiction

Understanding Fiction

As the creator of fiction, you want to be able to tell a story that is worthwhile and will engage your audience.

Every good fiction book comes with:

- A creative imagination;
- An original idea;
- A strong narrative;
- Characters that people can relate to, disapprove of, or admire;
- An ability to look beyond reality and enter a world of vision, fantasy, and invention.

Questioning the narrative

It is important that, after reading the text, you think about what has been said.

You need to be able to read an extract from a book, and understand the passage in further detail.

By asking questions as you go through, this will allow you to understand what the author was trying to say:

- How does the author want me to feel at this point?
- How does the author feel at this point?
- Why have I been provided this information?
- What can I learn from the information that has been provided?
- Why has the author used a particular phrase?
- Who is the narrator of the text and how are they being portrayed?

DAY 2 ➡ Understanding Fiction

STRUCTURE OF FICTION WRITING

All fiction writing will follow a similar structure, and have a beginning, a middle, and an end.

If you are creating your own story, or you are analysing the structure of a narrative, you should consider the following points:

- Setting, atmosphere and emotion;
- Characters and themes;
- Imagery and language.

In paper 1 of your English Language exam, you will be provided a piece of fiction, and you will need to be able to analyse this.

When it comes to analysing a text, you need to focus on a number of literary aspects.

- Literary fiction is mostly written with the intention to entertain the reader. This is done through a number of ways; making the reader feel emotional through the way a character is represented or how the atmosphere is presented.
- Fiction texts will use a range of descriptive and figurative language in order to enhance the writing and make the writing more imaginative.
- Dialogue is a great way for the plotline to progress by allowing the reader to get a sense of personal touch in relation to the characters.

DAY 2 ➡ Understanding Fiction

SETTING, ATMOSPHERE AND EMOTION

THE IMPORTANCE OF SETTING

The setting of a novel is one of the key elements in literary writing. When writing about settings, you can include descriptions on:

- Where the action takes place;
- What the weather is like;
- What time of day it is.

It is up to the reader how they picture the setting. Everyone visualises stories differently. One thing may look completely different to two different people.

Take a look at the pictures!

Both images are of a forest. However, they both look very different. The way this setting would be described would depend on what feelings, mood and atmosphere the writer was trying to create.

For example, in the first image, it could represent:

- Idealism;
- Peacefulness;
- Beauty.

However, the second image could represent:

- The unknown;

DAY 2 → Understanding Fiction

- Fear;
- Isolation.

TYPES OF EMOTIONS

The type of emotion that is conveyed in the narrative will depend on what genre the story is from. It will also depend on what is happening at the time (i.e. what action is currently taking place in the narrative?)

There are a whole range of emotions that writers can convey in their writing. This might include some of the following:

Anger	Desire	Wonder	Sorrow
Fear	Guilt	Happiness	Joy
Shame	Love	Envy	Courage
Hope	Confusion	Relaxation	Ghostly

CREATING AN ATMOSPHERE AND ADDING EMOTION

When writers describe a setting, they are trying to create a particular mood or atmosphere.

When looking at atmosphere, you should look at:

- What feelings/moods are created?
- How does the atmosphere tie in with the action?
- How does the atmosphere tie in with the narrative?

Different atmospheres created in a story will make the reader feel different things. The writing needs to make the reader feel a certain way in order for them to feel engaged with the narrative.

DAY 2 ➔ Understanding Fiction

CHARACTERS AND THEMES

EVERY GREAT STORY NEEDS GREAT CHARACTERS

The characters of a story are extremely significant, as they allow the reader to follow the lives of made-up individuals. The way in which a character comes across to readers is through characterisation.

The way a character is characterised can be through:

- The way they look;
- The way they speak;
- The way they dress;
- The way they act.

THE IMPORTANCE OF THEMES

An author will use one or more themes in their story to emphasise particular ideas.

The genre and narrative of the story will depend on what themes occur.

Below we have listed some of the most common themes:

Love	Hate	Revenge	Jealousy
Justice	Power	Conflict	Childhood
Coming of Age	Struggle	Poverty	Family
Friendship	Death	Courage	Discovery
Ambition	Alienation	Freedom	Fear

Themes are a great way to draw upon emotions.

For example:

- The theme of love connotes happiness and romance;

DAY 2 ➡ **Understanding Fiction**

- The theme of death connotes sadness, anger, and isolation.

Some themes can tie in with one another:

- The theme of childhood can also be linked to memories;
- The theme of poverty can also be linked to struggle.

IMAGERY AND LANGUAGE

IDENTIFYING IMAGERY

When we talk about imagery, it is not always used in a literal sense. More often than not, writers use imagery as a way of describing something in a symbolic way.

Writers will use particular words and phrases to emphasise a particular idea or image in order to create a picture in the reader's imagination.

When looking at imagery, you should ask yourself the following questions:

1. What is the image?
2. How and why is it effective?
3. Can it be interpreted in another way?

There are two main ways that an author can create effective imagery:

SIMILES   **METAPHORS**

DAY 2 → Understanding Fiction

UNDERSTANDING SIMILES

A simile is a sentence that describes something "as" or "like" or "than" something.

> She was as white as a ghost.

> My brothers were fighting like cat and dog.

She was as white as a ghost.

- The simile compares the appearance of a girl to a ghost.
- The use of the word "as" describes one thing like something else.

My brothers were fighting like cat and dog.

- The simile compares the behaviour of two boys to a cat and dog fighting.
- The use of the word "like" describes the boys' behaviour being similar to the behaviour of a cat and dog fighting.

What similes can you think of?

DAY 2 ➡ **Understanding Fiction**

UNDERSTANDING METAPHORS

A metaphor is a sentence where one thing is called something else. In other words, it is a figure of speech in which a word or phrase is applied to something else, which is not literally applicable.

> Life is a roller coaster.

> Their bedroom is a zoo.

Life is a roller coaster.

- The metaphor suggests that life has its ups and downs.
- It is comparing life to a roller coaster.
- The fact that it doesn't use the words "as" or "like", means it is a metaphor, and not a simile.

Their bedroom is a zoo.

- The metaphor suggests that their bedroom is a mess and/or chaotic.
- It is comparing a bedroom to a zoo.
- The fact that it doesn't use the words "as" or "like", means it is a metaphor, and not a simile.

<u>What metaphors can you think of?</u>

DAY 2 ➡ Understanding Fiction

GETTING TO GRIPS WITH LANGUAGE

Authors are able to get extremely creative in their writing, and tend to use literary techniques to create a certain effect.

There are lots of different literary techniques which can be used – each using language in a different way in order to create meaning or effect.

Below are some of the key literary techniques that you should familiarise yourself with:

Personification	Repetition	Hyperbole
Emotive language	Onomatopoeia	Pathetic fallacy
Oxymoron	Rhetorical question	Alliteration
Symbolism	Assonance	Colloquialism
Tautology	Bathos	Irony

DAY 2 ➡ Understanding Fiction

Day 2 Checklist

You have now completed your Day 2 revision.

How confident are you feeling?

Below we have included a checklist that you can tick off to make sure that you have learnt everything regarding this chapter.

I have read and understood the different types of fiction. ☐

I have fully grasped the structure of fiction writing. ☐

I feel confident enough to write about setting, atmosphere, and emotion. ☐

I feel confident enough to write about charactres and themes. ☐

I feel confident enough to write about imagery and language. ☐

I feel confident in tackling any question relating to fiction texts. ☐

DAY 2 ➡ Checklist

UNDERSTANDING NON-FICTION
Day 3

STRUCTURE OF NON-FICTION WRITING

Non-fiction texts are based on facts as opposed to made-up stories or imaginative ideas.

Our whole world uses loads of examples of non-fiction which are all used for different purposes and/or audiences.

Below we have outlined some key examples of non-fiction literary texts:

- Adverts;
- Letters;
- Reviews;
- Essays;
- Diary entries and/or blog entries;
- Newspaper articles;
- Magazine articles;
- Autobiographies;
- Leaflets.

In paper 2 of your GCSE English Language exam, you will be provided a sample of a non-fiction text. This may take any form and you will need to analyse the text.

DAY 3 ➔ Understanding Non-Fiction

ESSAY WRITING

Essays are a great way to structure your writing.

Essays are a form of writing which allow you to answer a question.

WHAT ALL GOOD ESSAYS NEED

All good essays need a clear and focused structure. You can achieve this by creating an introduction, a middle, and an end.

INTRODUCTION
- Outline what direction your essay is going to take.
- You could include a hypothesis.
- Use keywords from the question.
- 2-3 sentences is sufficient for an introduction.
- The reader should be able to read your introduction and conclusion, and know what your essay is about.

MAIN BODY
- Answer the question by making 3-4 points.
- Support these points with examples, quotes and analysis.
- Make sure you keep referring to the question.
- 3-4 paragraphs is sufficient for an essay.
- Analyse and explain key points, their relevance and your opinions.

CONCLUSION
- Summarise the key points you've made and how they are important/relevant.
- DO NOT introduce any new points in the conclusion.
- Make sure you write a sentence referring to the question.
- The reader should be able to read your introduction and conclusion, and know what your essay is about.

On the next few pages, we have created a template which you can use and redraw to help you when it comes to structuring your essays. We've also provided a sample essay, and highlighted key points throughout the essay.

As well as structure, essays also need to flow, use effective language, use the correct tone, and of course, answer the question.

ESSAY FEATURES	EXPLANATION
Language	Consider what language is best. For essays, formal and technical language is great. Use long, fancy words only if you know the meaning of them.
Tone and Style	You need to set the tone. Is it serious or light-hearted? Your language should reflect this.
Paragraphing	Use a paragraph for each new point. Your introduction and conclusion will form paragraphs, and then you'll have 3 or 4 paragraphs for your main body.
Literary Techniques	Avoid repetition. Rhetorical questions are great to interact your reader. Consider what techniques you can use to enhance your writing.

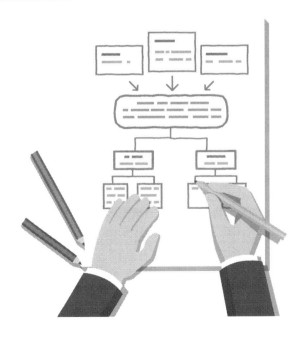

DAY 3 ➔ **Understanding Non-Fiction**

Understanding Non-Fiction

KEY WORDS AND PHRASES

For each section of your essay, we have provided some key words and phrases that you could use for each part.

INTRODUCTORY WORDS
- In this essay
- We are introduced to
- Within this essay
- I am going to

OPINIONATED WORDS
- I believe
- I think
- I am convinced
- My opinion
- My point of view
- I feel
- It seems that

TRANSITION WORDS
- First/second/third
- Consequently
- Although
- Equally important
- In addition
- Obviously
- Furthermore
- Additionally

CONCLUSION WORDS
- In conclusion
- Finally
- In summary
- Overall
- We can see that

DAY 3 → Understanding Non-Fiction

QUESTION

INTRODUCTION

MAIN BODY 1

MAIN BODY 2

MAIN BODY 3

IMPORTANT QUOTES / KEYWORDS

CONCLUSION

DAY 3 → Understanding Non-Fiction

STORY WRITING

Story writing is a great way for you to get creative.

USE A PLAN

All great stories start with a simple idea. This idea is then expanded upon, using descriptions, imagery, and language.

Plans are a great way to structure what you want to say.

THE IMPORTANCE OF ORIGINALITY

Every good story comes from a simple idea. However, that idea needs to demonstrate some originality. What is going to make your story different from everyone else's?

Take an idea and make it your own; add a twist or unusual event which makes it different from stories that have already been told.

TELLING A STORY

When you are telling a story, it is important to pay particular attention to the following:

- Language;
- Structure;
- Tone;
- Characters / Characterisation;
- Setting;
- Narrative;
- Audience.

KEEPING YOUR READER ENGAGED

Right from the offset, your story needs to be exciting. The beginning of your story needs to be able to keep the reader's attention.

DAY 3 ➡ **Understanding Non-Fiction**

Nobody will want to keep reading if the story starts out as boring, and doesn't improve.

STRUCTURING YOUR WRITING

With every great story, comes a well-thought out structure of events.

The way in which a story pans out has carefully been crafted by the author. The author wants to hook you in right from the start; they want to use action and events to keep you thoroughly entertained, and they want an ending that is original and fitting to the rest of the narrative.

That is why an introduction, a middle and an end are extremely important!

To better your writing, you will need to undergo practice; the more practice you do, the better your writing will become.

Remember, writing is all about finding your voice!

STRUCTURING YOUR STORY

The first thing you need to understand is that the structure of your story is important. It allows the reader to be engaged instantly, and be kept excited until the very end.

Understanding Non-Fiction

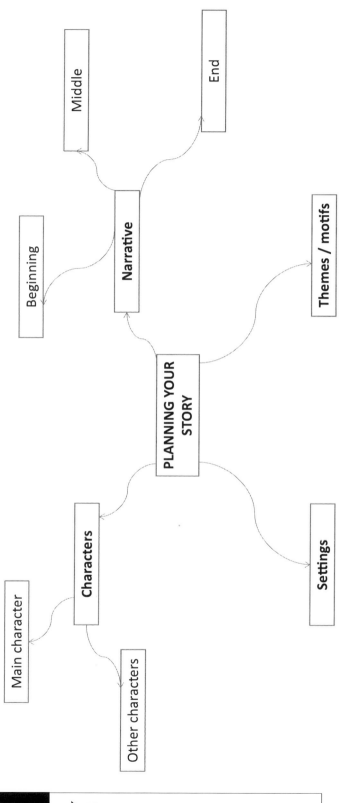

DAY 3 → Understanding Non-Fiction

LEAFLETS

Leaflets are a form of writing that provides lots of information about a certain topic.

One of the main features of leaflets is not just the content and the language, but the layout. The layout helps enhance the appeal of the leaflet by making people want to pick the leaflet up and read it.

Below is a list of features that leaflets need in order to be appealing:

- Have a clear, interesting title;
- Use sub-headings in order to break up the information;
- Use bullet points in order to break up the information;
- Images are a great way to make the leaflet more easy on the eye.

It is unlikely that you will be asked a question in the exam about leaflets. However, it is great practice to get in the swing of things and learn the ins-and-outs about what a good leaflet includes.

Below is an example of a leaflet

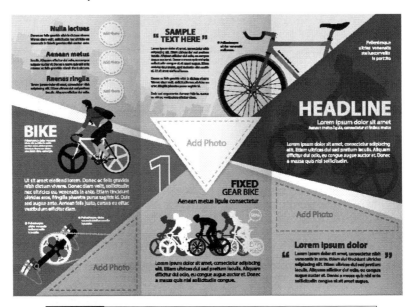

DAY 3 ➡ Understanding Non-Fiction

LETTERS

Letters can be a handwritten or printed document which can be used for many purposes:

- Written letters to family or friends;

- Formal letters which can be a letter of complaint or a letter of resignation.

Letters need to be structured in a very particular way. You will need to look at the audience of the letter before deciding on the tone that your letter will take.

Below we have outlined a few key features that you should consider when writing letters:

- Use formal greetings to begin and end your letter. For example, 'Dear Sir/Madam' and 'Yours Sincerely'.

- If your letter is taking a formal approach, remember to use Standard English. Avoid abbreviations and slang terminology.

- If your letter is taking a less formal approach; addressing a friend or relative for example, you may wish to write your letter in a more conversational style, rather than being too wordy and formal.

DAY 3 → **Understanding Non-Fiction**

REVIEWS

Reviews provide feedback and opinions about anything. From a concert to a restaurant to purchasing products, reviews are a great way to read about other people's experience with the same thing.

Reviews can be used for many reasons:

- To inform;
- To describe;
- To entertain;
- To analyse;
- To advise.

For more information on the purpose of writing, see the following chapters:

- *Argue, persuade and advise*
- *Explain, inform and describe*

REVIEW OF ROMEO AND JULIET (the last night)

After reading great reviews about the opening night, I had psyched myself up for a night full of conflict, love, violence and poetry.

However, this "noble attempt" did not live up to my expectation. The modern-day twist which was put on the classic love story simply did not work.

The characters were abysmal and put in little effort. Maybe they were tired from all their shows, or maybe their acting was just not up to par with what I would expect from professionals.

DAY 3 ➡ Understanding Non-Fiction

NEWSPAPER ARTICLES

Newspaper articles are a great example of a non-fiction text. Newspaper articles come in different forms:

- News reports;
- Featured articles;
- Editorials;
- Opinion pieces.

Newspaper articles come in two different types of newspaper style – tabloids and broadsheet.

TABLOIDS

- Tabloids tend to use shorter sentences and use less complicated vocabulary.
- Tabloid reports are sensationalized, meaning that they appeal to reader's emotions through the use of language.
- Examples of tabloids include The Daily Mirror and The Sun.

BROADSHEETS

- Broadsheet newspapers will use longer, more complicated sentences and paragraphs in order to appear more advanced.
- The tone takes a much more formal approach in comparison to tabloids.
- Broadsheets focus on significant national and international issues.
- Examples of broadsheets include The Times and The Telegraph.

Below is an example of a typical newspaper layout. It uses images, headings and sub-headings in order to break up the text and make it easier to read.

UNEXPLAINED OBJECT
IN BRITISH SKIES

A BIZARRE, UNIDENTIFIED object was once again reported soaring the skies right here in Britain.

Two reports were made on the very same day and were claimed to have happened just minutes apart. Paranormal experts and scientific investigators are staggered by this profound event, and are furthering their inquiries.

The first incident was reported at 08:16am on Wednesday, and the unnamed witness claims to have been "fetching her daily newspaper" when the extraordinary thing happened. She claims that she's "never seen anything like it" and "had to look twice".

A flying object, which was described by both witnesses as being triangular-shaped, was caught flying through the skies over the countryside in Lenham, Kent.

The next reporting was at 09:32am, 2 miles south from the first location.

Sammie Harris, 26, and her husband, Daniel, 29, were driving back to their house, when they both looked out the passenger-side window. Sammie pulled over the car, and they both stepped out.

"It was a flat object, a light colour, which drifted through the air. Like a shooting star falling from the sky, the object appeared to be heading downwards", Daniel claimed, with both nerves and excitement in his voice.

"If my husband had not been there, I don't think anyone would have believed me". Sammie was unsure what she saw at first, and when she pointed it out to Daniel, they both came to the same conclusion.

All of the witnesses described the object as having a slight yellow tinge to it, which flashed in time with a regular heartbeat.

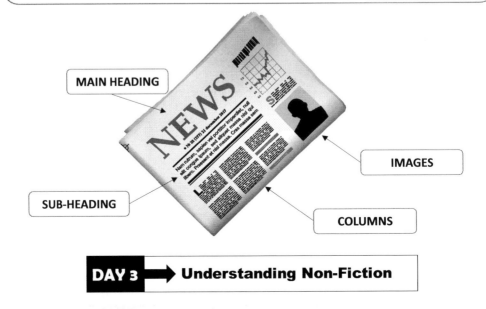

DAY 3 → Understanding Non-Fiction

DIARIES

Diaries are a personal account of thoughts, feelings and/or events. They are often written in a chronological order over a prolonged period of time.

Below we have included a few features of diary writing:

- Diaries should be personal. They are often written in first person in order to convey the writer's point of view.

- The language used in a diary is often informal and creative. It can use slang language in order to create a personal account of events.

- The tone can vary. Depending on the purpose of the entry will depend on what tone is used.

Below we have included an example diary entry taken from the Diary of Anne Frank between 1942 and 1944.

> **August 21st 1942:** *"Now our Secret Annex has truly become secret. Because so many houses are being searched for hidden bicycles, Mr. Kugler thought it would be better to have a bookcase built in front of the entrance to our hiding place. It swings out on its hinges and opens like a door. Mr. Voskuijl did the carpentry work. (Mr. Voskuijl has been told that the seven of us are in hiding, and he's been most helpful.) Now whenever we want to go downstairs we have to duck and then jump. After the first three days we were all walking around with bumps on our foreheads from banging our heads against the low doorway. Then Peter cushioned it by nailing a towel stuffed with wood shavings to the doorframe. Let's see if it helps!"*

SPEECHES

Speeches are a great way to create powerful and emotive writing. Speeches need to be emotive in order to have an effect on the audience.

Listed below are different reasons why a speech might be given:

- To persuade;
- To argue.

Speeches need to maintain a clear and effective structure. This will allow the speech to be fluent and progress with emotion and excitement.

Speeches often use lots of literary techniques that we have discussed in the Grammar, Punctuation and Spelling chapter.

Below we have provided an example of a speech. In your exam, you may be required to write a speech for paper 2 of your English Language GCSE. Take a look at the The Queen's 1957 Christmas broadcasted speech.

> *Happy Christmas.*
>
> *Twenty-five years ago my grandfather broadcast the first of these Christmas messages. Today is another landmark because television has made it possible for many of you to see me in your homes on Christmas Day. My own family often gather round to watch television as they are this moment, and that is how I imagine you now.*
>
> *I very much hope that this new medium will make my Christmas message more personal and direct.*

DAY 3 ➡ Understanding Non-Fiction

Day 3 Checklist

You have now completed your Day 3 revision.

How confident are you feeling?

Below we have included a checklist that you can tick off to make sure that you have learnt everything regarding this chapter.

I have read and understood the different types of non-fiction. ☐

I have fully grasped the structure of non-fiction writing. ☐

I feel confident enough to analyse essays and stories. ☐

I feel confident enough to analyse leaflets, letters, and reviews. ☐

I feel confident enough to analyse newspaper articles, diary entries, and speeches. ☐

I feel confident in tackling any question relating to fiction texts. ☐

DAY 3 ➡ **Checklist**

WORKS OF SHAKESPEARE
Day 4

THE WORKS OF SHAKESPEARE

WHO WAS WILLIAM SHAKESPEARE?

William Shakespeare was a British poet and playwright, and is still considered one of the greatest writers in literary history.

To be, or not to be: That is the question

SHAKESPEARE AND HIS WORK

Shakespeare wrote around 40 plays, 154 sonnets and a whole range of other poetry about 400 years ago (1564-1616).

Some of his most well-known plays include:

ROMEO AND JULIET	MACBETH	JULIUS CAESAR
A MIDSUMMER NIGHT'S DREAM	OTHELLO	THE TAMING OF THE SHREW
MUCH ADO ABOUT NOTHING	KING LEAR	HAMLET

The works of Shakespeare are taught in schools as a way of recognising writing that is in an old-fashioned style.

Due to the time in which Shakespeare was writing (over 400 years ago), his writing style was very different to how we read and write today.

DAY 4 ➡ Works of Shakespeare

Shakespeare's works were able to capture the interest of his audience using conflict and emotion.

LIVING IN SHAKESPEAREAN TIMES

Obviously, there are many differences between the era in which Shakespeare was writing, and now.

Shakespeare's writing was heavily influenced by what life was like. This enabled him to appeal to his audiences, by conveying similar imagery and values which were recognisable.

The key areas that Shakespeare paid particular attention to when writing are listed below.

Government

- For the majority of his life, Shakespeare grew up writing under the reigning monarch of Queen Elizabeth I;
- King James I ruled after her.

Religion

- England was a Christian country;
- Almost everyone believed in God and went to church;
- Many people believed in witchcraft, magic, and ghosts;
- No-one divorced in this era.

Women

- Women had no rights;
- They had to obey what their father (and/or husband) told them;
- Women had no career opportunities;
- They were often forced into arranged marriages;

DAY 4 → Works of Shakespeare

- Even if the woman was the eldest, the first eldest brother would inherit everything.

Education

- Boys (from the age of 4) would go to school to learn, to read, and write;
- They would also learn prayers, teachings of the Church, and working with numbers;
- Grammar schools would focus on Latin, translations and writing;
- Girls would stay at home and learn to be domesticated (cook, sew, music). Only a few girls would learn to read and write.

Health

- Diseases were prominent around the city of London;
- The Black Death (also known as the Plague) wiped out thousands of civilians;
- Many children died from the disease, including Shakespeare's son, Hamnet.

Class

- At the time of writing, society was divided into different classes;
- These classes defined people's wealth and status, which ultimately formed a hierarchy which people would follow;
- The nobles (considered the very richest of people) were called 'lords' and 'ladies'. They were the ruling class, which had influence over what the monarchy did;
- Just beneath the nobles, were the gentry. These people were rich

DAY 4 ➡ Works of Shakespeare

enough to survive off their own wealth, but did not have titles within society;

- Shakespeare himself was raised as a middle class citizen. The middle class consisted of yeomen, merchants, and craftsmen. Whilst they were not wealthy, they lived comfortably, and their children would have gone to school;

- The lower class worked for the superiors in society. The lower class had little money, but were still able to attend the theatre.

FEATURES OF SHAKESPEARE'S WORK

Shakespeare used a range of literary techniques in order to appeal to his readers/audiences.

There are three main areas that you should focus on when reading Shakespeare:

- *Language;*
- *Characters;*
- *Themes.*

LANGUAGE

Many people struggle to understand the works of Shakespeare, because his writing style and language is extremely different to ours.

The use of old-fashioned language made it difficult for readers to interpret, but these words and phrases were often worked out by understanding the rest of the script.

For example:

The following extract is the opening from Othello.

> **RODERIGO**
>
> | | |
> |---|---|
> | Tush, never tell me! I take it much unkindly | *Don't try and make me believe that* |
> | That though, Iago, who hast had my purse | *Have* |
> | As if the strings were thine shouldst know of this. | *Talking about the elopement.* |

Getting used to the language is difficult, but with more practice, this will become easier.

Remember, you don't have to understand every word in order to understand what is being said. Some of the words are simply missing letters, whilst others are words that you might not have heard of!

You will need to be able to translate what is being said, in order to analyse what is being said.

<u>Things to look out for:</u>

Words that you may not recognise or words that were used in a different context to how they would be used today.

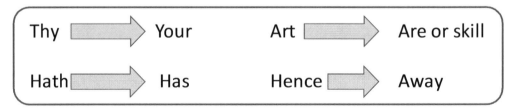

| Thy | ⟹ | Your | Art | ⟹ | Are or skill |
| Hath | ⟹ | Has | Hence | ⟹ | Away |

The language used was often quite 'wordy'. Words and phrases were often swapped around which makes it tricky to work out what is actually being said.

When you read Shakespeare's plays, it is important to read straight into the next line (unless there is a full stop or other punctuation mark).

In a lot of Shakespeare's works, he used poetic devices in his dialogue. Poetry was often spoken by the characters who were wealthy, whereas slang and normal language were spoken by the commoners.

Works of Shakespeare

Shakespeare used language to emphasise religious, biblical, medical, legal, and sexual references.

> Full fathom five thy father lies;
> Of is bones are coral made;
> Those are pearls that were his eyes:
> Nothing of him that doth fade
>
> *The Tempest*

CHARACTERS

Characters play a crucial role in the works of Shakespeare. They are often conveyed to the audience in a particular way, in order to create different emotions and ideas about each character.

When you read about characters, you need to consider the following:

- *How do they act?*
- *What is their role in the narrative?*
- *What do they get up to?*
- *How do they speak?*
- *What is their relationships like with other characters?*
- *How does Shakespeare want you to feel about that character?*

Take a look at the representation of a few characters from Romeo and Juliet:

CHARACTER	REPRESENTATION
Romeo	• Impulsive, immature, devoted, passionate • His dialogue towards Juliet is very poetic, deep and meaningful
Juliet	• Naive, innocent, devoted • Lack of freedom • Shows courage and independence
Friar Lawrence	• Friend to both Romeo and Juliet • Civic-minded • Tries to create union between the two families
The Nurse	• Sentimental character • Confidant to Juliet • A comical character

THEMES

What is the play about? What is the overall theme of the play?

Shakespeare wrote loads of plays, each of which focussed on different key themes. These themes were all considered relevant to the time in which Shakespeare was writing.

There are three types of Shakespearean plays:

1. Comedies
2. Tragedies
3. Histories

Comedies

- This is a different type of humour than what we find funny in today's world.
- Most Shakespearean comedies offer dramatic storylines, alongside their underlying humour.

- Most comedies offer a happy ending.

Characteristics = struggle of young love, element of separation, mistaken identities, interwoven plotlines, use of puns and irony, and family conflict.

Tragedies

- Tend to be more serious, dramatic, and tense.
- Usually involve death of main character/s.

Characteristics = social breakdown, isolation of main characters, ends in death, noble characters who are brought down by their flaws, and no escape from the drama.

Histories

- Focus on English monarchs including King John, Richard II, Henry VIII and more.
- Dangers of civil war and conflict.
- Present a particular image of monarchs, although often considered as misrepresentations and inaccurate.

Characteristics = use of English monarchs to centre the storyline, glorify ancestors, depict monarchs in a particular way, and use conflict and tragedy to dramatise the narrative.

Listed below are some common themes that appear across the works of Shakespeare.

LOVE	FORBIDDEN LOVE	FAMILY	FRIENDSHIP
MORALS	RELIGION	RIVALRY	HONOUR
INNOCENCE	REVENGE	FATE	JUSTICE
SLAVERY	MAGIC	BETRAYAL	FORGIVENESS

Generally, plays will have more than one theme running through the narrative.

Some themes may be more obvious than others.

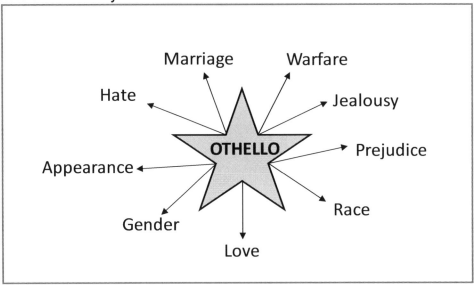

DAY 4 ➡ **Works of Shakespeare**

AUDIENCES

William Shakespeare's works appealed to the majority. Just like today, ticket prices were based on whereabouts you sat.

Shakespeare wanted to target a mass audience, from merchants and nobles, to poorer people.

When it comes to reading the works of Shakespeare, it is important that, as the reader, you are able to understand how Shakespeare appealed to his audience.

In his works, Shakespeare used language, imagery, themes, characters, and narrative to appeal to his targeted audience.

THEATRE PERFORMANCES

As we all know, plays are meant to be performed. So when reading Shakespeare's plays, keep in mind that they are meant to be performed on stage.

This will allow you to analyse the play in more detail, highlighting how this would have been effective for a Shakespearean audience.

The folllowing is a list of facts that you should try to remember for your GCSE exam:

INTERESTING FACTS!

- If the audience didn't like the play, they would throw apples at the actors.
- Women were not allowed to act. All female roles were played by men. This is evident in Shakespeare's comedies, as he often references this in a jokey manner.
- The costumes for the plays were often quite elobarate to highlight the fashion of that time.
- The settings of plays were often kept minimalistic to ensure that they were easily adapted for each scene.
- The only person who didn't go to the theatre was Queen Elizabeth I.
- People who stood to watch the play were called 'groundlings'. In the summer, they would be referred to as 'stinkards'.
- Merchants would buy tickets to sit in the boxes next to the stage.
- Nobles would buy seats on the stage because they could be seen by everyone.

DAY 4 ➡ Works of Shakespeare

SHAKESPEAREAN LANGUAGE

Of course, we cannot provide you with all of Shakespeare's unusual Elizabethan words. However, we thought we would provide you with some of the most popular words and translations, in order to become familiar with the kind of language Shakespeare used.

We have also provided space for you to fill in words yourself to see whether or not you are able to translate old-fashioned English into modern-day English. As you read through works of Shakespeare, if there are any words you are unsure of, write them down and get a friend, parent or teacher to help you translate it.

Remember to use this glossary when revising to ensure you know what Shakespeare is talking about.

MODERN DAY	ELIZABETHAN
Afraid	Afeard
Aware	Acknown
Away	Hence
Banished	Banish'd
Before	Ere
Beg	Pray
Chase (romantically)	Woo
Come here	Come hither
Curse	Plague
Days	-morrow
Desire	Will
Does	Doth
Enemy	Foe
Escaped	'scap'd
Farewell	Adieu

DAY 4 → **Works of Shakespeare**

Go	Hie
Go away	Avaunt
Has	Hath
Have	Hast
Here	Hither
Indeed	Marry
Inferiors	Sirrah
I think	Methinks
It is	'tis
Ignore	Shun
Kill	Dispatch
Listen	Hark
Misery	Woe
Never	Ne'r
No	Nay
Nothing	Nought
Often	Oft
Order	Charge
Pay attention	Mark
Quickly	Apace
Remember	Bethink
Sad	Heavy
Soon	Anon
There	Thither
To which	Whereto
Were	Wast
Why	Wherefore
Wished	Wish'd
Yes	Aye

DAY 4 ➔ **Works of Shakespeare**

Modern Day	Elizabethan
You	Thou; thee
You are	Thou art
You should	Thou should'st
Your	Thy

MODERN DAY	ELIZABETHAN

DAY 4 ➔ Works of Shakespeare

Now that we have provided some example of Shakespearean words and phrases, let's take a look at some key literary techniques.

GETTING TO GRIPS WITH SHAKESPEAREAN LANGUAGE

LITERARY TECHNIQUE	EXAMPLE
Simile	"Oh, he sits high in all the people's hearts, / And that which would appear offense in us, / His countenance, like richest alchemy." (Julius Caesar)
Metaphor	"In time the savage bull doth bear the yoke." (Much Ado About Nothing)
Personification	"And flecked darkness like a drunkard reels." (Romeo and Juliet)
Repetition	"I'll have my bond; I will not hear thee speak: I'll have my bond; and therefore speak no more...I'll have no speaking: I will have my bond." (The Merchant of Venice)
Hyperbole	"The raven himself is hoarse that croaks the fatal entrance of Duncan under my battlements." (Macbeth)
Emotive language	"Did my heart love till now? Forswear its sight! for I ne'er saw true beauty till this night." (Romeo and Juliet)
Onomatopoeia	"Cock-a-diddle-dow" (The Tempest)
Dramatic irony	"I will go before, sir. Mistress, look out at window, for all this: There will come a Christian boy, will be worth a Jewess' eye." (The Merchant of Venice)

DAY 4 ➔ Works of Shakespeare

Works of Shakespeare

When talking about the above literary techiques, consider:

- *Why the author has chosen to use the technique?*
- *What impact does this have on the reader/audience?*
- *What does this say about the character?*
- *How does this impact the narrative?*

> In The Tempest, the character, Ariel, uses lots of examples of onomatopoeia to emphasise animal imagery. Other characters also use this literary technique – the association of animal imagery with Caliban could be symbolic of Prospero's attitude towards him.

> Romeo's emotive speech towards Juliet clearly emphasises the importance of love and desire. When Romeo uses the rhetorical question of "did my heart love till now?" this shows how Shakespeare often uses poetry techniques to highlight the power of love between the protagonists.

THE IMPORTANCE OF HUMOUR

When analysing language, Shakepeare often uses humour in his works. Puns and jokes are often demonstrated in the hope to keep with the theme of the story, relieve tension and drama, and to lighten and uplift the mood of the reader/audience.

Let's explore this idea further using a couple of examples:

> In Romeo and Juliet, when Romeo asks Mercutio how badly wounded he is, he says "Tis not so deep as a well, nor so wide as a church-door, but 'tis enough, 'twill serve... Ask for me tomorrow, and you will find me a grave man." Mercutio's use of the word "grave" not only suggests how serious his wounds are, but also signifies the resting place of the dead. His jokey language about his own death demonstrates Shakespeare's humour to help lighten the mood.

DAY 4 ➡ Works of Shakespeare

> Mercutio's humour in Romeo and Juliet comes across as being rude, sexual and bitter. Mercutio uses sexual innuendos towards the Nurse. His words of "Tis no less, I tell you, for the bawdy hand of the dial is now upon the prick of noon," highlights sexual connotations. This would have been humorous for a Shakesperean audience.

SHAKESPEARE'S USE OF POETRY IN DRAMA

Shakespeare often used poetry techniques in his plays.

Things to look out for:

1. Does the character's speech change between prose and poetry?
2. Remember, if a new line starts with a capital letter it is **VERSE**, if it continues from the last line, it is **PROSE**.

When you quote verse, it is important that you show that the quote continues over a line using the slash symbol '/'.

> In Macbeth, the witches speak in verse. Not only does this set them apart from other characters, but also creates a poetic, musical feel. "Double, double, toil and trouble / Fire burn and cauldron bubble." This uses rhyming couplets to highlight the poetic technique even further. Shakespeare does this to create a light-hearted atmosphere on a topic (witchcraft) that would have been quite scary for Shakespearean audiences.

Day 4 Checklist

You have now completed your Day 4 revision.

How confident are you feeling?

Below we have included a checklist that you can tick off to make sure that you have learnt everything regarding this chapter.

I have read and understood the different works of Shakespeare. ☐

I have understood the importance of theatre performances. ☐

I am improving my knowledge with regards to Shakespearean language. ☐

I understand the reasons why Shakespeare uses poetry in his drama writing. ☐

I feel confident in tackling any question relating to Shakespearean literature. ☐

DAY 4 ➡ Checklist

ANALYSING POETRY
Day 5

ANALYSING POETRY

Everyone reads and responds to poetry in different ways. However, despite there being many ways to read and interpret a poem, there are four things that can help break down the poem clearly:

- Language;
- Form;
- Structure;
- Poetic Techniques.

Before we move on and talk about the aforementioned in more detail, we think the best place to start is with your personal response.

Personal response

When you read a poem, think about the effect it has on you. Questions to consider include:

- *How does the poem make you feel?*
- *What is the poem about?*
- *What parts of the poem stand out? Why?*
- *What position does the poet take?*
- *Are there multiple ways of interpreting the poem?*

PAPER 2

> Compare the ways poets present ideas about power in 'Storm on the Island' and one other poem from 'Power and Conflict'.

- This question focuses on the theme of power.
- The question is asking you to "compare", which means that you

need to look at more than one poem.

- Using poetic techniques including language, structure and form, analyse the poem and explore how the poet wants the reader to feel.

- With regards to personal response, you should try to explain how the poem makes YOU feel.

Types of poems

Below is a list of the types of poems you will be expected to know for your assessments.

 Sonnet
Lyrical
14 lines
10 syllables to a line
Often about love

 Narrative
Tells a long story
Voice of narrator
or character
Do not have to rhyme

 Tanka
Originate in Japan
5 lines
Syllable count of 5 / 7 / 5 / 7 / 7
Use of similes, metaphors or personification

 Limerick
5 lines
Lines 1, 2 and 5 rhyme
Lines 3 and 4 rhyme
To make you laugh

 Cinquain
5 lines
'Cinq' = 5 in French
Syllable count of 2 / 4 / 6 / 8 / 2

 Couplet
2 lines for a verse
Both lines rhyme

 Haiku
Originate in Japan
3 lines
Syllable count of 5 / 7 / 5
Often about nature

 Acrostic
Word written vertically
Each letter starts sentence
All lines should relate
to the topic of the poem

 Ode
Ancient Greece
Lyric poem
Praise of a person or thing
Deep feelings or emotions

 Free Verse
Follows no rules
Rhythm, syllables, number of lines,
topic = can be anything

STRUCTURE, FORM AND LANGUAGE

When it comes to your exam, it is important to identify the keywords in the question. This will help you to tailor your response and ensure you answer the question sufficiently.

Identifying keywords

Below are examples of keywords and phrases that could appear in your exam. Provided below is advice on how to approach each 'type' of exam question.

Question Type	Keywords and phrases	Approaching the question	Considerations
Comparison	Compare / contrast / identify similarities and differences.	Use two or more poems to show how they are similar and how they differ.	Compare throughout your answer. Try to avoid writing about each poem seperately.
Understanding a poem	The way in which the poem / poet...	Analyse themes, form, structure, and language. Link to effect.	What and how does the poem get its message across.
Approaching the exam	Explore / discuss / write about / conside.	Analyse the poem by exploring techniques. Offer personal responses.	Consider how the poem can be read differently. Offer your response.

Now that we've had a look at the types of poems and questions you could face during the exam, let's go back to looking at language, form and structure.

Analysing Poetry

LANGUAGE	Look at the words that have been used. Why do you think the poet has used those particular words? Analyse imagery and poetic techniques – how do these create meaning?
FORM	When we talk about form, we mean the number of lines a poem has or the rhyme scheme. What type of poem is it? Why is this important to the narrative or theme of the poem?
STRUCTURE	Structure is all about how the poem is moulded together. Think about how the poet arranges their ideas and themes in the poem. Is there a particular reason something is done?

Different forms of poetry

As mentioned previously, there are different forms (types) of poems. Each form uses different rules and this allows us to identify what type of poem we are reading.

Take a look at some of the most common forms of poetry:

- **SONNETS** = 14 lines in length, with a regular rhyming pattern (often in iambic pentameter). Usually lines contain 10 syllables, and uses rhyming couplets.

  An example of a sonnet in your exam is Sonnet 29 by Barrett Browning.

- **FREE VERSE** = Irregular in length and has no set rhythm pattern. The poem does not have to rhyme, although it can. Do not follow any rules with regards to poetry techniques.

DAY 5 → Analysing Poetry

An example of a free verse poem in your exam is **Poppies** by Weir.

- **DRAMATIC MONOLOGUES** = narrated by one person (distinct from the poet) which addresses an implied audience.

An example of a dramatic monologue in your exam is **Porphyria's Lover** by Barrett Browning.

These are just a few examples of types of poetry. Of course, there are many more and you will be given lots of different types of poems in the exam.

When it comes to form, you need to have knowledge of some poetic terminology.

STANZA (VERSE)	TERCET	QUATRAIN
a group of lines	a three-line stanza	a four-line stanza
COUPLET	RHYMING COUPLET	RHYMING TRIPLET
pair of lines, with the same metre	a couplet where the final words on each line rhyme	final words on three successive lines rhyme

Let's take a look at an example:

> In Porphyria's Lover, the poet uses a rhyming couplet which provides rhythm. For example, "And all night long we have not stirred / And yet God has not said a word!" This sounds triumphant despite the act of killing Porphyria, suggesting God accepted this as being morally correct.

The importance of structure

The way in which a poem is structured is important to the overall arrangement of the poem's content.

The poet will arrange their ideas, themes and feelings in a particular way in order to convey them in the most effective manner.

Generally speaking, a poem will use four main aspects for structure:

- Stanza;
- Rhyme;
- Meter;
- Line breaks.

We've already discussed stanza and rhythm, but let's quickly take a look at the terms 'meter' and 'line breaks'.

Meter	This is the rhythmic structure of a poem. Sometimes you can work this out by tapping along to the syllable count.
Line Breaks	A line break is where a line of poetry ends. This causes for the reader to pause which determines how the poem is read.

> One summer evening (led by her) I found
> A little boat tied to a willow tree
> Within a rocky cove, its usual home.
>
> The Prelude: Stealing the Boat by William Wordsworth

- Can you see how the poem is structured?

- Wordsworth has purposefully used line breaks in his poem to signify where to pause. This creates quite a dramatic effect for its readers as it allows them to stop and think about the line before continuing with it.

DAY 5 ➡ Analysing Poetry

In the exam, analysing a poem's structure is vital to scoring top marks. When looking at structure, consider the following questions:

1. How does the poem start?

2. How does the poem end?

3. Does the voice of narration change throughout the poem?

4. Is there a change in rhythm, mood and pace?

5. Does the poet use line breaks to create pauses and interruptions. Why do you think they do this?

6. How many stanzas does the poem have? Does this have an impact on the reader?

7. What rhyming schemes are used throughout the poem? Do they change? Why do you think the poem has chosen to use this rhyming scheme in particular?

8. How do YOU as the reader feel when reading the poem? Does your opinion change by the end of the poem? If so, why do you think the poet has done this?

The importance of language

One of the biggest things to remember when writing or analysing poetry is the use of language.

Poets will use specific language in order to create meaning. The best way for poets to create meaning through language is to use literary techniques.

The next few pages comprise of different poetic techniques that you should learn prior to your exam. Being able to spot these techniques during the exam will really help you to develop your analysis and ultimately score more marks.

POETIC TECHNIQUES

ALLITERATION

Definition	Alliteration involves repeating the same initial in the same line.
Example	"With hay, so as you can see, there are no stacks / Or stooks that can be lost" (Storm on the Island, Seamus Heaney)
Effect	The alliteration of "stacks" and "stooks" stresses the importance of solidarity and strength of togetherness.

ASSONANCE

Definition	Assonance is the repetition of vowel sounds in nearby words.
Example	"The poignant misery of dawn begins to grow... / We only know war lasts, rain soaks" (Expose, Wilfred Owen)
Effect	The assonance of the 'oh' sound in "grow", "know" and "soaks" reinforces the mood of the poem. This signifies a pessimistic, painful process of awakening.

DAY 5 → **Analysing Poetry**

COLLOQUIALISM

Definition	The use of informal language which is often used in everyday speech.
Example	*"When us was wed she turned afraid"* (The Farmer's Bride, Charlotte Mew)
Effect	This use of colloquialism is used to indicate a lack of education and sophistication. This gives the poem a simplistic feel. By doing so, this ties in nicely with the theme of 'farmers' which are supposedly less-educated and working class.

ENJAMBMENT

Definition	The continuation of a sentence without a pause beyond a line or stanza.
Example	*"He was running / Like a man who has jumped up in the dark and runs / Listening between his footfalls for the reason / Of his still running"* (Bayonet Charge, Ted Hughes)
Effect	The sentence emphasises a quick-fast paced narration. The soldier is running towards danger. The enjambment between these lines add to the flow and pace of the poem. This allows the poet to create a sense of speed and adrenaline.

HYPERBOLE

Definition	Hyperboles are exaggerated statements in order to make something seem more excessive than it actually is.
Example	*"Nothing beside remains. Round the decay / Of that colossal Wreck"* (Ozymandias, Percy Bysshe Shelley)
Effect	The hyperbole in the use of the word "colossal" highlights the sheer scale of the destruction of an empire. This emphasises the consequences of ones actions on a catastrophic scale, which allows the reader to view the King's "works" as worthless and cataclysmic.

IMAGERY

Definition	The use of visually descriptive or figurative language.
Example	*"Small circles glittering idly in the moon, / Until they melted all into one track / Of sparkling light."* (The Prelude, William Wordsworth)
Effect	This description allows the reader to have a clear visualisation of the poem's setting. The poet uses words such as "glittering" and "sparkling" to create a sense of peace, serenity and perfection.

DAY 5 ➡ Analysing Poetry

IRONY

Definition	Irony is a way of using words or phrases in which the intent of those words actually carries the opposite meaning. Irony does not always have to be taken negatively. Some poets often use a form of irony that allows the reader to overlook the meaning, and understand different attitudes or conflicting interpretations.
Example	*"Which yet survive, stamped on these lifeless things"* (Ozymandias, Percy Bysshe Shelley)
Effect	Shelley uses an ironic contradiction to show how everything the king owned is dead, and only nature remains. This reinforces the idea of loss of power, and the idea of human vs. nature.

METAPHOR

Definition	Another figure of speech which uses a word or phrase to describe an object or action, which is not literally appropriate.
Example	*"In his darkroom he is finally alone / with spools of suffering set out in ordered rows"* (War Photographer, Carol Ann Duffy)
Effect	A 'spool' is the cylinder on which the film is wound i.e. a reel. The use of this word works as a metaphor for grievance and pain. The reel contains pictures of war victims, which emphasises the negative mood.

ONOMATOPOEIA

Definition	These are words that sound like what they are describing.
Example	*"Northward, incessantly, the flickering gunnery rumbles"* (Exposure, Wilfred Owen)
Effect	The line in the poem creates a distinctive rhythmic pattern. The use of onomatopoeia on the words "gunnery" and "rumbles" creates the illusion of echos and continuity.

OXYMORON

Definition	A figure of speech where two contradictory terms appear in conjunction (i.e. bitter sweet).
Example	*"Exploding comfortably"* (Storm on the Island, Seamus Heaney)
Effect	Heaney uses this oxymoron to show that he is used to the sounds of a storm and therefore feels comfortable. While most people would think that 'exploding' and 'comfortably' contradict one another, Heaney sees storms as familiar, and as a part of life.

PERSONIFICATION

Definition	Using human characteristics to describe inanimate objects. Giving objects or 'things' feelings or emotions, or human attributes.
Example	*"The waterlogged earth / gulping for breath"* (Winter Swans, Owen Sheers)
Effect	This suggests that the earth has opened and has become soft; the couple sinks with every step. Not only does this convey an outdoor setting, but could signify how nature and humans are alike.

REPETITION

Definition	Repeating a word or phrase. This is done in order to emphasise key themes or ideas.
Example	*"But nothing happens"* (Exposure, Wilfred Owen)
Effect	This is a repeated line throughout 'Exposure'. This suggests that Owen believes that soldiers' actions were pointless. Although the soldiers might believe that their actions are having no effect, the irony is that something actually is happening...the soldiers are slowly dying. This ties in with the theme and mood of the poem.

RHYME

Definition	The repetition of similar sounding words. This is mostly done with the end words of sentences.
Example	*"Three Summers since I chose a maid, / Too young maybe – but more's to do / At harvest-time than bide and woo."* (The Farmer's Bride, Charlotte Mew)
Effect	The rhyme scheme of the first stanza is a-b-b-a-c-d-c-d-d. This allows the reader to read at a fluent pace and get a sense of rhythm and flow.

SIMILE

Definition	A simile is a figure of speech which compares one thing to another. The reason for this is to make the image more vivid and descriptive.
Example	*"Like boats righting in rough weather"* (Winter Swans, Owen Sheers)
Effect	This describes how the swans put themselves back up into swimming position. This connotes the idea of stability. Even in a storm, swans are able to find their way and keep their balance.

DAY 5 → Analysing Poetry

Day 5 Checklist

You have now completed your Day 5 revision.

How confident are you feeling?

Below we have included a checklist that you can tick off to make sure that you have learnt everything regarding this chapter.

I have read and understood the importance of poetry, and how to analyse texts. ☐

I have understood different structures, forms, and languages used in poetry. ☐

I have learned all of the key poetic techniques. ☐

I feel confident in tackling any question relating to poetry. ☐

DAY 5 ➡ Checklist

19TH AND 20TH CENTURY PROSE
Day 6

In this chapter, let's quickly recap what you can expect in terms of your GCSE English Literature exam, including 19th Century and 20th Century Prose.

The 19th Century Novel

During the 19th Century novel section of your English Literature exam, you will be required to answer **ONE** question.

Students will study one novel within the classroom, so the choice of question you should answer should be the one you have been focusing on during your English lessons.

In the exam, there will be a choice of seven novels. The following texts are examples taken from the 2017 examination:

- *The Strange Case of Dr Jekyll and Mr Hyde;*
- *A Christmas Carol;*
- *Great Expectations;*
- *Jane Eyre;*
- *Frankenstein;*
- *Pride and Prejudice;*
- *The Sign of Four.*

PLEASE NOTE: The choice of 19th Century texts are subject to change annually. Be sure to check with your teacher with regards to the novel that you will be studying!

Modern Texts

During the modern text section of your English Literature exam, you will be required to answer **ONE** question.

Students will study one text within the classroom, so the choice of question you should answer should be the one you have been focusing on during your English lessons.

In the exam, there will be a choice of twelve texts, including post-1914 prose and drama. The following texts are examples taken from the

2017 examination:

PROSE

Author	Title
William Golding	Lord of the Flies
AQA Anthology	Telling Tales
George Orwell	Animal Farm
Kazuo Ishiguro	Never Let Me Go
Meera Syal	Anita and Me
Stephen Kelman	Pigeon English

DRAMA

Author	Title
JB Priestley	An Inspector Calls
Willy Russell	Blood Brothers
Alan Bennett	The History Boys
Dennis Kelly	DNA
Simon Stephens	The Curious Incident of the Dog in the Night-Time
Shelagh Delaney	A Taste of Honey

PLEASE NOTE: The choice of modern texts is subject to change annually. Be sure to check with your teacher with regards to the novel/play that you will be studying!

Day 6 Checklist

You have now completed your Day 6 revision.

How confident are you feeling?

Below we have included a checklist that you can tick off to make sure that you have learnt everything regarding this chapter.

I have read and understood different 19th and 20th century prose. ☐

I know what to expect in my upcoming GCSE exam. ☐

EXAM PRACTICE
Day 7

GRAMMAR, PUNCTUATION, AND SPELLING

QUESTION 1

For each of the sentences below, circle whether the sentence is active or passive.

1. The horrific fire destroyed the rainforest.

2. The cricket ball was thrown by Phillip.

3. The principal examined students' school reports.

QUESTION 2

Underline ALL of the adjectives in the sentences below.

1. Tyrone was wearing a black, chequered jacket.
2. Simon was a curious boy.
3. It was the most bizarre feeling.
4. The fragile, lonely woman sat recumbent in her bed.

QUESTION 3

Circle whether to use the pronoun 'I' or 'me' in the following sentences.

a) My brother and _____ went on holiday (me, I)

b) Is this really happening to _____? (me, I)

c) Carrie and _____ love playing hockey. (I, me)

QUESTION 4

Circle the two words that are in the correct tense, in order for the sentences to read correctly.

a) The celebrity _____ hundreds of autographs and then _____ to call it a day.

   DECIDE   SIGN   SIGNED   DECIDES   DECIDED

b) Abbie's mum told her if she _____ her homework, she _____ be able to watch some TV before bed.

   FINISH   WILL   WILL HAVE   WOULD   FINISHED

c) The runner _____ to catch up with her opponent but she couldn't. However, the runner _____ beat her personal best.

   TRY   TRIED   DO   DOES   DID

QUESTION 5

Tick the box if the sentence is punctuated correctly.

a) I like playing football and tennis. ☐

b) "What is the time, said Pete". ☐

c) However, I did not expect that. ☐

d) My teacher, Miss Day, was the best English teacher at school. ☐

e) Even though I was unprepared, I passed with flying colours. ☐

QUESTION 6

Below is a list of homonyms. In the space provided, write down two different meanings of how that word can be used.

HOMONYM	MEANING 1	MEANING 2
Ring		
Rock		
Row		
Duck		
Chest		

SHAKESPEARE

The Tempest

This extract is taken from **Act III Scene I**. Ferdinand has been set to work by Prospero.

> **FERDINAND**
>
> There be some sports are painful, and their labour
>
> Delight in them sets off: some kinds of baseness
>
> Are nobly undergone and most poor matters
>
> Point to rich ends. This my mean task would be as heavy to me as odious,
>
> But the mistress which I serve quickens what's dead
>
> And makes my labours pleasures: O, she is ten times more gentle than her father's crabbed
>
> And he's composed of harshness. I must remove
>
> Some thousands of these logs and pile them up,
>
> Upon a sore injunction: my sweet mistress
>
> Weeps when she sees me work, and says, such baseness
>
> Had never like executor. I forget:
>
> But these sweet thoughts do even refresh my labours, most busy lest, when I do it.

QUESTION 1

Explain how Shakespeare presents Ferdinand.

Write about:

- How Shakespeare presents Ferdinand in this extract;
- How Shakespeare presents Ferdinand in the overall play.

OR

The Merchant of Venice

This extract is taken from **Act IV Scene I**. Antonio and Shylock are summoned before the court.

> What if my house be troubled with a rat,
>
> And I be pleased to give ten thousand ducats
>
> To have it baned? What, are you answered yet?
>
> Some men there are love not a gaping pig,
>
> Some that are mad if they behold a cat,
>
> And others when the bagpipe sings i'th'nose
>
> Cannot contain their urine; for affection,
>
> Mistress of passion, sways it to the mood
>
> Of what it likes or loathes...
>
> ...
>
> So can I give no reason, nor I will not,
>
> More than a lodged hate and a certain loathing
>
> I bear Antonio, that I follow thus
>
> A losing suit against him. Are you answered?

QUESTION 2

Explain how Shakespeare presents the relationship between Antonio and Shylock.

Write about:

- How Shakespeare presents the characters in the extract;
- How Shakespeare presents the characters in the overall play.

19TH CENTURY NOVEL

A Christmas Carol (Charles Dickens)

This extract is taken from **Stave 3**. Scrooge meets the Ghost of Christmas Present.

> Scrooge entered timidly, and hung his head before this Spirit. He was not the dogged Scrooge he had been; and though the Spirit's eyes were clear and kind, he did not like to meet them.
>
> "I am the ghost of Christmas Present," said the Spirit. "Look upon me!"
>
> Scrooge reverently did so. It was clothed in one simple green robe, or mantle, bordered with white fur. This garment hung so loosely on the figure, that its capacious breast was bare, as if disdaining to be warded or concealed by any artifice. Its feet, observable beneath the ample folds of the garment, were also bare; and on its head it wore no other covering than a holly wreath, set here and there with shining icicles. Its dark brown curls were long and free; free as its genial face, its sparkling eye, its open hand, its cheery voice, its unconstrained demeanour, and its joyful air.

QUESTION 1

Explain how Dicken's portrayal of the ghosts plays a significant part in A Christmas Carol.

Write about:

- how Dickens presents the ghost in this extract;
- how Dickens presents the ghosts in the novel overall.

OR

Great Expectations (Charles Dickens)

This extract is taken from **Chapter 3**. Magwitch thanks Pip for the food brought to him.

> "Well," said he, "I believe you. You'd be but a fierce young hound indeed, if at your time of life you could help to hunt a wretched warmint hunted as near death and dunghill as this poos wretched warmint is!"
>
> Something clicked in his throat as if he had works in him like a clock, and was going to strike. And he smeared his ragged rough sleeve over his eyes.
>
> Pitying his desolation, and watching him as he gradually settled down upon the pie, I made bold to say, "I am glad you enjoy it."
>
> "Did you speak?"
>
> "I said I was glad you enjoyed it."
>
> "Thankee, my boy. I do."
>
> I had often watched a large dog of ours eating his food; and I now noticed a decided similarity between the dog's way of eating, and the man's. The man took strong sharp sudden bites, just like the dog. He swallowed, or rather snapped up, every mouthful, too soon and too fast; and he looked sideways here and there while he ate, as if he thought there was danger in every direction of somebody's coming to take the pie away. He was altogether too unsettled in his mind over it, to appreciate it comfortably I thought, or to have anybody to dine with him, without making a chop with his jaws at the visitor. In all of which particulars he was very like the dog.

QUESTION 2

Explain how Dickens presents Magwitch as being a pitiful character.

Write about:

- how Dickens presents Magwitch in this extract;
- how Dickens presents Magwitch in the novel overall.

MODERN TEXTS

Q1

How does Russell use the characters Mrs Johnstone and Linda to represent women in *Blood Brothers*?

Write about:

- How Russell represents women;
- How Russess explores gender differences.

Q2

How is fatherhood explored in *The Curious Incident of the Dog in the Night-Time*?

Write about:

- How Stephens writes about Christopher's father;
- How language and plot are used to develop the reader's understanding of Christopher's father.

POETRY

Compare how poets present power in *Storm on the Island* and in **one** other poem from '*Power and Conflict*'.

We are prepared: we build our houses squat,

Sink walls in rock and roof them with good slate.

This wizened earth has never troubled us

With hay, so, as you see, there are no stacks

Or stooks that can be lost. Nor are there trees

Which might prove company when it blows full

Blast: you know what I mean - leaves and branches

Can raise a tragic chorus in a gale

So that you listen to the thing you fear

Forgetting that it pummels your house too.

But there are no trees, no natural shelter.

You might think that the sea is company,

Exploding comfortably down on the cliffs

But no: when it begins, the flung spray hits

The very windows, spits like a tame cat

Turned savage. We just sit tight while wind dives

And strafes invisibly. Space is a salvo,

We are bombarded with the empty air.

Strange, it is a huge nothing that we fear.

UNSEEN POETRY

How Do I Love Thee? (Sonnet 43)

> How do I love thee? Let me count the ways.
> I love thee to the depth and breadth and height
> My soul can reach, when feeling out of sight
> For the ends of being and ideal grace.
> I love thee to the level of every day's
> Most quiet need, by sun and candle-light.
> I love thee freely, as men strive for right.
> I love thee purely, as they turn from praise.
> I love thee with the passion put to use
> In my old griefs, and with my childhood's faith.
> I love thee with a love I seemed to lose
> With my lost saints. I love thee with the breath,
> Smiles, tears, of all my life; and, if God choose,
> I shall but love thee better after death.

Elizabeth Barrett Browning

How does Barrett Browning present the concept of love in 'How Do I Love Thee?'

READING

This extract is taken from a short story written in 2018 by How2Become.

My city. The beautiful backstreets bustle, and the gorgeous alleyway aroma drifts and flows and fills my nostrils, as I scamper, satisfied, along the cold stone pavements. I feel a rush of warmth inside of me as I catch glimpse of my friends. I see their nude tails whip violently, excitedly, around the corner and I scurry to catch them. To be reunited once again with Todd, Marsha, George and oh…there's my brother, Harry. Why did he have to be here? Regardless, we have the gang all together again, like it should be.

We all pause for a moment to catch precious breath and I look up at the people above. They look empty, like hollow marching clones, clumping and thumping their enormous bodies around, drifting aimlessly into one brightly lit shop after another. I strain my eyes staring for so long in a seemingly timeless daze that yellows and reds and blues start to merge into one strange aura of colour and light, and I lose all awareness of the commotion around me.

I don't think I will ever tire of living here. At least that's one thing I can be sure of. As for my friends, I eventually snap myself out of my hazy restful state to find that they have completely deserted me. Not to worry, I think, I'm fine here on my own at the moment. I do seem to have a habit of losing myself in my own thoughts, only to find that everyone else has already long gone.

As I continue to make my way down the street, I decide to have a bit of fun. I start to dodge in and out of people's feet and legs, even sometimes accidentally brushing my tail gently against them. This makes them scream with terror. Sometimes they jump up and run away, and I watch them as they disappear into the distance. I really don't know what it is about me that induces such a reaction, but I guess bigger isn't always better. I rule this city. No doubt.

I quickly dart back into the familiar alley to escape from the people's voices.

The drones, the piercing laughter, it is all starting to get a bit much for me. Dinner. What's on the menu tonight? Every night is a surprise for me, I can tell you that! No ordering and waiting for hours on end, no deliberating over this and that. No, I'm not a time waster. Life is too short, as they say. I know, I know – it's a cliché but it's entirely true. At least in my opinion. Got to experience everything you possibly can, meet people. I cross paths with the type of personalities that spark my imagination in this city every single day.

Finding something to eat proves more difficult than it sounds tonight. To be honest it does seem to be getting a lot tougher as of late. All I want is something small, just to tickle my stomach. Although I wouldn't say no to a warm, hearty meal – haven't had one of those in a while. Still, I go on. Must be the early hours of the morning by now. The city never sleeps, eh? Well I certainly do. I delight in curling up in the deliciously pungent sewer.

I pick my favourite spot to settle down and find Marsha and Todd already resting close by. We eventually all fall asleep to the disappointed rhythms of our empty, rumbling stomachs. Sounds like they haven't had much luck with dinner tonight either.

Within minutes of drifting off, the intense pang in my stomach wakes me again. This sort of thing seems to be turning into a routine just lately. The pain is sharper than usual this time, and every muscle in my body feels tired and sore. I plead with myself just to relax and drift back into sleep for probably an hour, to no avail.

I decide to have a bath to try and ease the aches and pains and help me relax a little more. I indulge in a thick, warm bath in one of my favourite corners of the sewer. I admittedly feel a little better but as soon as I step out I realise that the relief was short-lived. I eventually give in and decide that I will have to force myself up and head back into the city on another mission for nutrition.

I should probably have asked my friends to come with me this time. Many hands make light work as they say. I didn't want to wake them, though, and I'm not sure where my brother or George are. I'll probably end up bumping into one of them in one of our usual spots. The trouble for us is that people seem to be throwing away less and less. The streets are tidier, and the bins are emptier. It may be a nicer environment for the humans – but do they ever think of how it affects us?

QUESTION 1

Read the previous extract and note down 4 instances of the author's description of the city.

-
-
-
-

QUESTION 2

How does the writer use language to describe the narrator?

You could include the writer's choice of:

- Words and phrases;
- Language techniques;
- Sentence structure and form.

WRITING

QUESTION 1

Write a description suggested by this picture:

SUGGESTED COMMENTS

GRAMMAR, PUNCTUATION, AND SPELLING

Question 1

1. Active
2. Passive
3. Active

Question 2

1. Tyrone was wearing a <u>black, chequered</u> jacket.
2. Simon was a <u>curious</u> boy.
3. It was the most <u>bizarre</u> feeling.
4. The <u>fragile, lonely</u> woman sat <u>recumbent</u> in her bed.

Question 3

a) My brother and I went on holiday.
b) Is this really happening to me?
c) Carrie and I love playing hockey.

Question 4

a) The celebrity **signed** hundreds of autographs and then **decided** to call it a day.
b) Abbie's mum told her if she **finished** her homework, she **would** be able to watch some TV before bed.
c) The runner **tried** to catch up with her opponent but she couldn't. However, the runner **did** beat her personal best.

Question 5

The boxes you should have ticked were a, c, d, and e.

Question 6

HOMONYM	MEANING 1	MEANING 2
Ring	A ring you wear on your finger	A boxing ring
Rock	A large stone	A movement – to move back and forth in a rocking motion
Row	An argument	A row of seats (line of seats)
Duck	An animal	To 'duck' down
Chest	A treasure chest	Part of the body

SUGGESTED COMMENTS

SHAKESPEARE

Question 1

- You can talk about how Ferdinand is in service to Prospero.

- Explore how Shakespeare uses Miranda to distract Ferdinand.

- You can explore how balance is conveyed in Ferdinand's speech in relation to Miranda.

- Ferdinand is represented as the character who often allows fate to take its course.

- The fact that he tries to win Miranda's father's approval, shows his persistence and pureity to win over Miranda and her family.

QUOTATIONS TO CONSIDER:

"Might I but through the prison once a day / Behold this maid. All corners else o'th'earth / Let liberty make use of"

- Ferdinand implies that as long as he can see Miranda, he will be free. This shows the desire and lust between these two characters.

"Oh you, / So perfect and so peerless, are created / Of every creature's best"

- This signifies the love and romance between Miranda and Ferdinand. He claims that Miranda has no rival in the world and that she's utter perfection.

"Weeping again the king my father's wrack"

- This represents Ferdinand as being a caring son. This ties in with how Shakespeare conveys him throughout the play – as being noble and sweet.

"I had rather crack my sinews, break my back, / Than you should such dishonor undergo".

- Again, this represents Ferdinand as being a noble and chivalrous character.

Question 2

- You can explore how Antonio and Shylock's relationship is based on animosity and mistrust.

- You can talk about Shylock's determination to seek revenge on Antonio.

- Shylock and Antonio's personal fued stems from an "ancient grudge".

- Discuss how Shylock's idea of justice is based on "an eye for an eye". This has religious connotations as it's taken from the Old Testament.

- Explore how Antonio and Shylock's characters are represented differently. For example, Antonio is the Merchant of Venice and makes money by trading costly goods. He is anti-Jewish, which means he is often portrayed as cruel towards Shylock.

- The fact that Antonio forces Shylock to convert to Christianity says a lot about his character. Explore whether you think he does this because he is passionate about his religion, or whether he merely seeks revenge.

SUGGESTED COMMENTS

QUOTATIONS TO CONSIDER:

"I hate him for he is a Christian; / But more for that in low simplicity / He lends out money gratis, and brings down / The rate of usance here with us in Venice".

- The disdain that Antonio possesses sets a dismal tone for the play.

"If a Jew wrong a Christian, what is his humility? Revenge. If a Christian wrong a Jew, what should his sufferance be by Christian example? Why, revenge!"

- This reinforces Shylock's belief that Christianity is hypocritical. What effect does this have on Shakespearean audiences vs. audiences of today?

"My daughter! O my ducats! O my daughter!... My ducats and my daughter!"

- When his daughter, Jessica, runs away, it appears that he is just as upset about losing his money as he is about losing his daughter. This might suggest that Shylock cares immensely about money. Does he really value his relationship with his daugher? Or does he value money more?

19TH CENTURY NOVEL

Question 1

- Discuss how the portrayal of the three ghosts offers the idea of choice.

- Scrooge is confronted with the choices he has made in the past. The Ghost of Christmas Past represents Scrooge throughout his life. His perception of life has been shaped by his feelings of sad, happy and sad. Why do you think the author has done this? What does this say about Scrooge as a character?

- Is Scrooge tortured by his past as a result of the realisation provided to him by the ghosts? Do you think Scrooge would have come to terms with this without the help of the ghosts? Thus, what is the significance of the ghosts?

- The description of the Ghost of Christmas Present in the extract signifies a sense of ideal and free, somewhat different to the representation of Scrooge.

- How are each of the ghosts portrayed? Why do you think Dickens does that? What effect would this have on a reader?

QUOTATIONS TO CONSIDER:

"Scrooge entered timidly, and hung his head before the Spirit"

- The fact that Scrooge automatically holds his head down before the Spirit suggests that he knows his behaviour has been far from exemplary.

"And on its head it wore no other covering than a holly wreath"

- This quote not only demonstrates tranquility and angel-like connotations, but it also carries religious imagery.

"The chain he drew was clasped around his middle...cash-boxes, keys, padlocks, ledgers, deeds and heavy purses"

- This suggests that the ghost is being used to signify how Marley's regrets and sins resulted in an early death.

SUGGESTED COMMENTS

- Dickens explores the idea that, with the help of the ghost, Scrooge can change his ways before it's too late.

Question 2

- A key aspect to discuss in your response is the idea of social class.

- Magwitch is described as being less than fortunate. What do you think a reader of today would feel? Would this be the same feeling as someone reading it when it was published?

- Analyse how Magwitch being an orphan creates a sense of longing. This is bound to have an emotional effect on the reader.

- Could Magwitch's poor start in life be the reason he is condemned to a life of a criminal?

- Pip comes to admire Magwitch, and this shows how characters respond to Magwitch's character. He is admired by a young boy, he accepts him as being noble and good.

- Does Dickens choose to send the message that criminals are just unlucky as opposed to being bad people?

QUOTATIONS TO CONSIDER:

"Pitying his desolation"

- This enforces how not only the reader feels pitiful for Magwitch, but other characters in the novel do too.

"I now noticed a decided similarity between the dog's way of eating, and the man's"

- Magwitch's character being compared to a dog suggests how Magwitch has little in his life, especially when it comes to food. His way of eating being compared to how a dog eats suggests that he just ravishes the food implying hunger and lack of human etiquette.

"Look'ee here, Pip. I'm your second father. You're my son. I've put away money, only for you to spend"

- The fact that Magwitch takes Pip under his wing and looks after him suggests to the reader that he is trying to change his ways. The reader feels a sense of admiration and pity for both the characters. Both have very little in the world, and use each other in a way to make them a stronger person.

MODERN TEXTS

Question 1

- The three women in the play all suffer at the hands of a male character. Mrs Johnston, Mrs Lyons, and Linda are either all let down by their husbands or long for affection from them.

- Russell represents women and men in very different ways. Why do you think he does this? Would this have something to do with the time in which it was written?

- Female characters are presented as being passive, whereas the male characters are conveyed as being domineering, active, and masculine.

- Mrs Lyons is represented as being a lonely character. She has a cold exterior and finds it difficult to show affection. Is this her actual personality

SUGGESTED COMMENTS

exterior and finds it difficult to show affection. Is this her actual personality or do you think her husband has something to do with why she behaves in this way?

- The women in the play demonstrate a strong motherly instinct. The over-protective mother of Mrs Lyons demonstrates this. This conforms to the stereotype of women, whereby they would be required to stay at home and look after the family. Mrs Johnston is also another character that demonstrates this. Not only does this signify stereotypes, but also implies a moral idea that contraception (back in that time) was considered unacceptable.

- Mrs Johnston is presented as being uneducated. Why do you think Russell chooses to present a female character in this manner?

- Poverty and entrapment are also key themes that are conveyed in *Blood Brothers*. How does this have an impact on both the characters in the play and the audience?

- The character of Linda is conveyed as being strong-willed and supportive of male characters. A kind, compassionate character, she also highlights a feisty and humorous persona. Does this say anything about gender?

Question 2

- Explore how we see Christopher and his father often disagreeing. What effect does this have on the audience/reader?

- The central theme of the play is family, its importance, its impact, and its nature.

- Compare how parenthood is portrayed between Christopher and his father, and Ed and Judy. Why do you think Stephens portrays different ideas about parenthood?

- How does Stephens portray love and tension between the characters of Christopher and his father? Why do you think this is done?

- The play takes a dramatic turn when Christopher finds out that his father lied to him about his mother dying, and admitting that he killed Wellington.

- How is parenting conveyed to the reader/audience? Are the readers/audience able to relate to what is being shown?

POETRY

Question 1

This question requires you to analyse the concept of love in *Sonnet 29* and a poem of your choice from *'Love and Relationships'*.

Below we have provided you with a breakdown analysis of *Sonnet 29* which you can use to tailor your response and analyse a poem of your choosing:

"I think of thee!"

- This could suggest that the speaker and her love are apart. The use of the exclamation mark could signify the strength of her love.

SUGGESTED COMMENTS

"twine and bud"

- This creates natural imagery. This could be used to signify a romantic, blossoming relationship between them.

"Put out broad leaves, and soon there's nought to see"

- This is an extended metaphor used to emphasise the longing of the speaker's passion – waiting for her husband's imminent arrival.

"I do not think of thee- I am too near thee"

- The caesura is used to create a pause for dramatic effect. This suggests that the speaker will find harmony and peace on the return of her husband.

"Rustle thy boughs and set thy trunk all bare, / And let these bands of greenery which insphere thee / Drop heavily down"

- This extended tree metaphor is used to reitterate this idea of natural beauty. The use of the word "sphere" suggests enternity which implies a long-lasting love.

UNSEEN POETRY

Question 1

This question requires you to analyse the concept of love in *How Do I Love Thee?*

Below we have provided you with a breakdown analysis of the poem which you can use to tailor your response and analyse the poem:

"How do I love thee? Let me count the ways"

- This suggests that there are multiple reasons as to why a person can love. This expresses an intense feeling of romance and passion.

- Browning's attempt to define love is explored using this rhetorical question. The reader is automatically drawn in by questioning the topic themselves.

"I love thee"

- This phrase is used as repetition and reflects the love the poet has for their lover. This is a common literary technique used in sonnets.

"My old griefs"

- The use of the word "my" highlights the fact that the poem is autobiographical.

Other things that you should discuss should be structure.

- This sonnet is traditional – it contains 14 lines, and often uses assonance (Faith) and (Praise) as a way of defining the perfect love.

- The poem uses a fairly regular rhyming scheme. For example "height" and "light", "breath" and "death". This creates a steady flow within the poem, which suggests that love is being defined as steady and calm.

SUGGESTED COMMENTS

READING

Question 1

1. "The gorgeous alleyway aroma drifts and flows"
2. "The streets are tidier"
3. "And I lose all awareness of the commotion around me"
4. "The drones, the piercing laughter, it is all starting to get a bit much for me"

Question 2

Below are a few things to discuss in your answer:

- Why do you think the author has used a first person narration?
- What effect does a first person narration have on a reader?
- Why do you think the length of each sentence is quite short and to the point?

WRITING

Question 1

Here is a sample response for the alternative question:

I crouched down next to the abandoned shack. One hour had passed since I left the restaurant. Eight days since I'd last been home. Four months since I found the body. Thirty-two-years since the day I was born, and about ten minutes until I died.

There was no sign of the man. It was time to go. I held my breath, pulled my head up and ran across the field. The lake teased me, moonlight and wind and black water tearing at the corners of my eyes, daring me to look behind.

I reached the fence. There were no gunshots. I sat down with my back against the wood and heaved into the wet grass. I was lightheaded, but I was alive. I pulled myself to my feet…and froze. Cold steel clicked against the side of my head.

A female voice spoke, calmly and clearly, 'Don't move.'

<u>Key features:</u>

- Sentence structure is clear and written well.
- You have used a variety of sentence types including subordinate clauses.
- Demonstrated a good use of punctuation, showing that you can use each punctuation mark correctly.
- Emphasise great literary writing by using the correct grammar and spelling. You need to be able to articulate yourself through words, structure, and punctuation.
- Your style and tone of writing needs to be well-fitted in regards to who your writing is addressing.
- The content of your writing needs to be relevant to the question being asked.

SUGGESTED COMMENTS

asked.

- Your writing needs to demonstrate the purpose of the text. Is your writing meant to persuade, discuss, analyse, or argue?

- Is your writing effective? Is it clear and concise? Is it well structured, well written and relevant?

Day 7 Checklist

You have now completed your Day 7 revision.

How confident are you feeling?

Below we have included a checklist that you can tick off to make sure that you have learnt everything regarding this chapter.

I have practiced all of the different types of exam questions provided in the guide. ☐

I have attempted the exam questions in exam-style (i.e. setting a time limit, no talking, or computers etc.) ☐

I have read and understood the suggested comments provided for each question. ☐

I feel confident in tackling my GCSE English exam. ☐

IMPROVE YOUR ENGLISH ABILITY!

  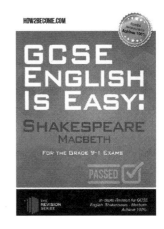

Our How2Become English revision guides are the ULTIMATE revision resources to prepare you fully for your English GCSE.

FOR MORE INFORMATION ON OUR GCSE GUIDES, PLEASE CHECK OUT THE FOLLOWING:

WWW.HOW2BECOME.COM

Get Access To
FREE
GCSE
TEST QUESTIONS

www.MyEducationalTests.co.uk

Printed in Great Britain
by Amazon